Mahatma Gandhi National Rural Employment Guarantee Act (MGNREGA)

Provisions, Implementation and Performance

Mahatma Gandhi National Rural Employment Guarantee Act (MGNREGA)

Provisions, Implementation and Performance

By

N.P. Abdul Azeez

Assistant Professor, Department of Economics,
Central University of Kashmir, Srinagar

and

S.M. Jawed Akhtar

Associate Professor, Department of Economics,
Aligarh Muslim University (AMU), Aligarh

New Century Publications
New Delhi, India

NEW CENTURY PUBLICATIONS
4800/24, Bharat Ram Road,
Ansari Road, Daryaganj,
New Delhi - 110 002 (India)

Tel.: 011-2324 7798, 4358 7398, 6539 6605
Fax: 011-4101 7798
E-mail: indiatax@vsnl.com • info@newcenturypublications.com
www.newcenturypublications.com

Editorial office:
LG–7, Aakarshan Bhawan,
4754-57/23, Ansari Road, Daryaganj,
New Delhi – 110 002

Tel.: 011-4356 0919

First Published: **2015**

ISBN: **978-81-7708-399-6**

Published by New Century Publications and printed at Salasar Imaging Systems, New Delhi.

Designs: Patch Creative Unit, New Delhi.

PRINTED IN INDIA

About the Book

Consistent with the approach for an employment-centred development strategy, public employment programmes are an integral part of planning and policy in India. Apart from the advantages that accrue to the unemployed, under-employed and the poorly-employed, such programmes have a positive macroeconomic impact via increase in effective demand from the hitherto poor and vulnerable segments of the population.

Mahatma Gandhi National Rural Employment Guarantee Act (MGNREGA), 2005 was notified on September 7, 2005. The Act came into force on February 2, 2006 when 200 selected districts of the country were brought under its purview (Phase I, 2006-07). MGNREGA was extended to additional 130 districts in Phase II during 2007-08. The remaining rural areas were notified with effect from April 1, 2008.

The objective of the MGNREGA is to enhance the livelihood security of unorganised workers in rural areas by guaranteeing 100 days of wage employment in a financial year to a rural household whose members volunteer to do unskilled manual work. The Act further aims at creating durable assets and strengthening the livelihood resource base of the rural poor. The choice of works suggested in the Act address causes of chronic poverty like drought, deforestation, soil erosion etc. so that the process of employment generation is on a sustainable basis.

This work traces the origin and development of MGNREGA and analyses its impact in rural areas in terms of Millennium Development Goals (MDGs), wage rate, financial inclusion, budgetary allocations, labour migration, governance and environmental concerns.

About the Authors

Dr. N.P. Abdul Azeez is currently Assistant Professor in the Department of Economics, Central University of Kashmir, Srinagar, Jammu & Kashmir. He was awarded gold medal for securing first position in M.A. (Economics) examination of Aligarh Muslim University (AMU), Aligarh. He has published a number of research papers in various reputed national and international journals and edited books. His areas of specialization include economics of rural development, and human resources management. He has participated and presented papers at various national and international conferences/seminars.

Dr. S.M. Jawed Akhtar is Associate Professor in the Department of Economics, Aligarh Muslim University (AMU), Aligarh, Uttar Pradesh. He was awarded gold medals for securing first position in B.A. (Hons.) and M.A (Economics) examinations of the same university. He has to his credit a good number of publications in various reputed national and international journals. He is an active member of several academic bodies.

Contents

Preface

Progressive reduction of unemployment has been one of the principal objectives of economic planning in India. It has been envisaged that the growth of the economy would not only increase production but also provide the capacity for absorbing the backlog of unemployment and under-employment and a substantial proportion of the additions to the labour force. The solution to the problem of unemployment—and the poverty that goes with it—has to be found ultimately through a high rate of overall economic growth. It is, therefore, necessary to have supplemental programmes for specific target groups/areas for employment creation, income generation and poverty alleviation. These have taken the form of direct employment programmes for providing seasonal employment to the agricultural labourers on rural capital works and infrastructure creation.

Consistent with the approach for an employment-centred development strategy, public employment programmes are an integral part of planning and policy. Apart from the advantages that accrue to the unemployed, under-employed and the poorly-employed, such programmes have a positive macroeconomic impact via increase in effective demand from the hitherto poor and vulnerable segments of the population.

Programmes to create direct employment opportunities for wage workers through public works have in the past focused on generation of supplementary employment opportunities, especially during lean periods. They have been considered as an important component of the anti-poverty strategy. These programmes are expected to create durable assets for the community and thus enhance further economic activities. Wage employment programmes also push up demand for labour and thus exert an upward pressure on the market wage rates by attracting people to public works programmes, thereby reducing supply of cheap labour, often at wages that would not even meet their bare basic needs.

Past experiences show that India's poverty alleviation

strategy—including the National Rural Employment Programme (NREP), Rural Labour Employment Guarantee Programme (RLEGP), Jawahar Rozgar Yojana (JRY), Employment Assurance Scheme (EAS), Sampoorna Gramin Rozgar Yojana (SGRY)—leaned towards wage employment programmes.

The rationale for adopting wage employment programmes by the Government during the last many decades has been that they provide steady opportunities for employment to those who are unemployed or under-employed. Beneficiaries include those who have labour as the only asset under their control (owning neither capital nor skills), and are unable to take even the minimal risks associated with self-employment. State assistance in the form of such wage employment then acts as a valuable safeguard against risks and vulnerabilities. Other positive externalities of wage employment programmes include the upward pressure on market wages because of the higher wages from the government programmes and organizing the rural poor beneficiaries of the schemes into collectives.

Mahatma Gandhi National Rural Employment Guarantee Act (MGNREGA), 2005 was notified on September 7, 2005. The Act came into force on February 2, 2006 when 200 selected districts of the country were brought under its purview (Phase I, 2006-07). MGNREGA was extended to additional 130 districts in Phase II during 2007-08. The remaining rural areas were notified with effect from April 1, 2008.

The objective of the MGNREGA is to enhance the livelihood security of unorganised workers in rural areas by guaranteeing 100 days of wage employment in a financial year to a rural household whose members volunteer to do unskilled manual work. The Act further aims at creating durable assets and strengthening the livelihood resource base of the rural poor. The choice of works suggested in the Act address causes of chronic poverty like drought, deforestation, soil erosion, etc. so that the process of employment generation is on a sustainable basis.

The significance of MGNREGA lies in the fact that it creates a right-based framework for wage employment programmes and makes the Government legally bound to provide employment to those who seek it. In this way the legislation goes beyond providing a social safety net, and towards guaranteeing the right to employment. By prioritizing natural resource management and emphasizing the creation of durable assets, it holds the potential of becoming a growth engine for sustainable development of an agriculture-based economy.

Under MGNREGA, employment is dependent upon the worker exercising the choice to apply for registration, obtain a job card and then to seek employment through a written application for the time and duration chosen by him/her. The legal guarantee has to be fulfilled within the time limit prescribed and this mandate is underpinned by the provision of unemployment allowance. The Act is thus designed to offer an incentive structure to the States for providing employment, as ninety percent of the cost for employment provided is borne by the Centre, and there is a concomitant disincentive for not providing employment, if demanded, as the States then bear the double indemnity of unemployment and the cost of unemployment allowance.

Earlier wage employment programmes were allocation-based. However, MGNREGA is not supply driven but demand driven. Resource transfer under MGNREGA is based on the demand for employment and this provides another critical incentive to States to leverage the Act to meet the employment needs of the poor. The delivery system has been made accountable, as it envisages an Annual Report on the outcomes of MGNREGA to be presented by the Central Government to the Parliament and to the State Legislature by the State Government.

MGNREGA is visualized as a first step towards the realization of the economic right to work as envisioned in the Directive Principles of State Policy in the Constitution of India. It recognizes Article 39 of the Constitution, according to which the State must ensure that "citizens, men and women equally, have the right to an adequate means to livelihood" and Article 41 whereby "the State, shall within the limits of its economic capacity and development, make effective provision for securing

Right to Work".

The potential of the MGNREGA to lead the economy towards a labour-intensive growth path needs to be emphasized in this context. The wage-work programme needs to be seen in a long-term perspective, with a strong planning component, dovetailing it with the ongoing development efforts, incorporating decentralised planning and implementation, skill training, maintenance of public assets and eventually absorbing wage-earners into mainstream employment. The path towards full employment lies in strengthening the sectors where the poor are located and stabilizing their incomes, improving their asset base, constructing basic socio-economic infrastructure at the local level, enabling access to paid work opportunities and exerting an upward pressure on market wages. MGNREGA as a programme is expected to create conditions for realisation of the above outcomes.

Srinagar
Aligarh
October 2014

N.P. Abdul Azeez
S.M. Jawed Akhtar

Abbreviations/Acronyms

AAY	*Antyodaya Anna Yojana*
ADS	Area Development Society
APL	Above Poverty Line
ATM	Automated Teller Machine
BCM	Business Correspondent Model
BPL	Below Poverty Line
CBS	Core Banking System
CDP	Community Development Programme
CDS	Centre for Development Studies
CDS	Community Development Society
CEGC	Central Employment Guarantee Council
CPI	Consumer Price Index
CRSE	Crash Scheme for Rural Employment
CSO	Central Statistical Organization
CV	Coefficient of Variance
DDP	Desert Development Programme
DPAP	Drought Prone Area Programme
DPC	District Programme Co-ordinator
DRD	Department of Rural Development
DWCRA	Development of Women and Children in Rural Areas
EAS	Employment Assurance Scheme
EGS	Employment Guarantee Scheme
FWP	Food for Work Programme
GDP	Gross Domestic Product
GP	*Gram Panchayat*
HDFC	Housing Development Finance Corporation
HDI	Human Development Index
HPI	Human Poverty Index
IAMR	Institute of Applied Manpower Research
IAY	*Indira Awas Yojana*
IBI	Index of Banking Inclusion
IRDP	Integrated Rural Development Programme
JGSY	*Jawahar Gram Samridhi Yojana*

JRY	*Jawahar Rozgar Yojana*
KSREGS	Kerala State Rural Employment Guarantee Scheme
KILA	Kerala Institute of Local Administration
LSG	Local Self-Government
MDG	Millennium Development Goal
MEGS	Maharashtra Employment Guarantee Scheme
MFAL	Marginal Farmers and Agricultural Labour Scheme
MGNREGA	Mahatma Gandhi National Rural Employment Guarantee Act
MGNREGS	Mahatma Gandhi National Rural Employment Guarantee Scheme
MIS	Management Information System
MPC	Marginal Propensity to Consume
MPCE	Monthly Per Capita Consumption Expenditure
MRD	Ministry of Rural Development
MSP	Malabar Special Police
NABARD	National Bank for Agriculture and Rural Development
NAC	National Advisory Council
NDP	Net Domestic Product
NFFWP	National Food for Work Program
NGO	Non-Governmental Organization
NHG	Neighbour Hood Group
NLM	National Literacy Mission
NREP	National Rural Employment Programme
NRHM	National Rural Health Mission
NRKs	Non-Resident Keralites
NRY	*Nehru Rozgar Yojana*
OMI	Out-Migration
PDS	Public Distribution System
PIREP	Pilot Intensive Rural Employment Programme
PMGSY	*Pradhan Mantri Gram Sadak Yojana*

PO	Post Office
PRIs	Panchayati Raj Institutions
PURA	Provision for Urban Amenities in Rural Areas
RBI	Reserve Bank of India
RGDWM	Rajeev Gandhi Drinking Water Mission
RIDF	Rural Infrastructure Development Fund
RLEGP	Rural Landless Employment Guarantee Programme
RMP	Rural Man Power
RNFE	Rural Non-Farm Employment
ROM	Return Out-Migration
RRB	Regional Rural Bank
RSBY	*Rashtriya Swasthya Bima Yojana*
RTI	Right to Information
SBT	State Bank of Travancore
SBI	State Bank of India
SC	Scheduled Caste
SD	Standard Deviation
SDP	State Domestic Product
SEGC	State Employment Guarantee Council
SFDA	Small Farmers Development Agency
SHG	Self-Help Group
SMGB	South Malabar Gramin Bank
SOR	Schedule of Rate
SPSS	Statistical Package for Social Science
ST	Scheduled Tribe
SGRY	Sampoorna Gramin Rojgar Yojana
SJGSY	*Swarna Jayanthi Grameen Swarozgar Yojana*
TPP	Twenty-Point Programme
TRYSEM	Training Rural Youth for Self-Employment
UNDP	United Nation Development Programme
UNICEF	United Nations International Children's Emergency Fund

1

MGNREGA and its Performance

1.1 Direct Employment Programmes

In countries where the economy is predominantly rural with agriculture absorbing the major share of labour force, broad-based rural development programmes holds the key to economic progress. Programmes to create direct employment opportunities for wage workers through public works have in the past focused on generation of supplementary employment opportunities, especially during lean periods. They have been considered as an important component of the anti-poverty strategy. These programmes are expected to create durable assets for the community and thus enhance further economic activities. Wage employment programmes also push up demand for labour and thus exert an upward pressure on the market wage rates by attracting people to public works programmes, thereby reducing supply of cheap labour, often at wages that would not even meet their bare basic needs.

Consistent with the approach for an employment-centred development strategy, public employment programmes are seen as an integral part of planning and policy. Apart from the advantages that would accrue to the unemployed, under-employed and the poorly-employed, such programmes have a positive macroeconomic impact via increase in effective demand from the hitherto poor and vulnerable segments of the population.

Past experiences show that India's poverty alleviation strategy—including the National Rural Employment Programme (NREP), Rural Labour Employment Guarantee Programme (RLEGP), Jawahar Rojgar Yojana (JRY), Employment Assurance Scheme (EAS), Sampoorna Gramin Rojgar Yojana (SGRY)—leaned towards wage employment programmes.

The rationale for adopting wage employment programmes by the Government during the last many decades has been that they provide steady opportunities for employment to those who are unemployed or underemployed. Beneficiaries include those who have labour as the only asset under their control (owning neither capital nor skills), and are unable to take even the minimal risks associated with self-employment. State assistance in the form of such wage employment then acts as a valuable safeguard against risks and vulnerabilities. Other positive externalities of wage employment programmes include the upward pressure on market wages because of the higher wages from the government programmes and organizing the rural poor beneficiaries of the schemes into collectives.

The solution of the problem of unemployment lies in reversing the causes of unemployment. It means controlling the population growth, speeding up the pace of industrialisation, adoption of labour-intensive technology and making the education system job-oriented.

Since the initiation of reforms in early 1990s, many changes have taken place in the social life and the institutions that govern the economy. In science and technology, information system and communications, revolutionary changes have occurred in recent times. New ideas have emerged which have changed the way people all over the world look at old ideas and the old institutions.

To deal with the unemployment problem, Government of India has launched, from time to time, various employment schemes. Huge amount of public money is being spent on recurring annual basis to support wage employment programmes. A constant monitoring of these programmes is necessary to evaluate their contribution to employment generation vis-à-vis expenditure incurred on them. The major programmes/schemes are explained below.

1.2 National Rural Employment Guarantee Act, 2005

The National Rural Employment Guarantee Act (NREGA) was enacted on August 23, 2005 and got presidential assent on

September 5, 2005 expressing the consensus of the state to use fiscal and legal instruments to address the challenges of unemployment and poverty. It came into force in 200 districts of India on February 2, 2006. It was "an Act to provide for the enhancement of livelihood security of the households in rural areas of the country by providing at least one hundred days of guaranteed wage employment in every financial year to every household whose adult members' volunteer to do unskilled manual work and for matters connected or incidental thereto" (NREGA, 2005).

Besides employment generation, the objective of the scheme is to create durable community assets for strengthening the livelihood source on a sustainable basis. It serves as a social safety net by providing a source of guaranteed employment—as such it is an "employer of last resort". It was initially called the National Rural Employment Guarantee Scheme (NREGS) but was rechristened on October 2, 2009 as Mahatma Gandhi National Rural Employment Guarantee Scheme (MGNREGA). The MGNREGA aims to achieve the twin objectives of rural development and employment. These two objectives are a landmark and milestone and would help to enhance human resources for inclusive growth. When the Act was passed, there was a fairly strong consensus that this was an initiative that would have the potential to transform rural India.

The national coalition government described MGNREGA as revolutionary, and maintained that it would have an impact on poverty in a major way by building infrastructure and enhancing growth in rural areas. Kannan (2005) has stressed that the potential of MGNREGA could be more fully realized if human development had been more fully prioritized, including, for instance, improved childcare facilities—which would help mothers to work under the scheme.

Thus, MGNREGA would lead to empowerment of various sections of society—the development of personal competencies and skills, to the process of challenging the existing power relations, household decision-making, gaining access, control over resources like credit, income, land, knowledge, and subjective variables like sense of personal power and self-efficacy'. The choice of works suggested in the Act addresses causes of chronic poverty like drought, deforestation and soil erosion, so that the process of employment generation is maintained on a sustainable basis. A well-designed employment guarantee programme can, under favourable circumstances, promote job creation, gender equality and pro-poor development.

MGNREGA has a great potential for increasing the volume of employment among the rural unemployed and underemployed. It provides ample opportunities for creating rural public assets, which has been largely neglected. It helps to enhance the purchasing power of rural households, thereby contributing to poverty alleviation. It also has the capacity to tap the hitherto under-utilized women labour force in rural India. By providing equal wages to both men and women, MGNREGA upholds the social position and integrity of women and thus promotes gender equality (Rania Antonopoulos, 2009).

MGNREGA can thus be considered as a timely intervention. Even after six decades of India's Independence, the country still fails to arrest abject poverty, illiteracy, malnutrition, social inequality and so on. A legal-binding rights based programme of this kind is expected to bring about a turnaround in the rural economy by eradication of all the above social malice. MGNREGA can improve sustainable rural livelihoods through spill-over effects, thereby enabling the poor to manage their risks and opportunities effectively. There is no denying of the importance of policy and programme actions for employment generation to ensure food security amongst poor than direct food subsidy strategies (Von Braun, 1995).

This 'employment of last resort' programme based on government expenditure would help in stabilizing and stimulating the economy by generating guaranteed employment. The rationale for these programmes is based on the premise that the government has an active role to play in promoting full employment in developing economies by assuming the role of the market maker for labour. An exploration on whether the MGNREGA has been able to fulfil its role of being the Indian version of the Keynesian scheme—like other schemes—brings about a lot of discussion on whether one should see it in the light of merely being an employment generation programme or one should perceive it as one which will impact the labour market drastically, providing an opportunity for labourers to not only demand for work but also demand for their right as a collective unit, under the banner of being a worker and not an individual, carrying social and political identity tags attached with their names.

This programme involves the establishment of a federally funded but locally decentralized job creation program as rural public work programme which secures an infinitely elastic demand for labour, ensuring simultaneously, full employment and price stability. The public works are supposed to play a positive role as income insurance due to the presence of seasonality in agrarian labour market (Basu, 2011), for building long-term capital assets (Basu, 1981), preventing dislocation of families in search of jobs and food (Dreze and Sen, 1991), and arresting rural-urban migration (Ravallion, 1999).

The Act is the most significant legislation of our times in many ways. For the first time, the power elite recognized the people's right to fight endemic hunger and poverty with dignity, accepting that their labour will be the foundation for infrastructure and economic growth. The rural communities have been given not just a development programme but a regime of rights.

MGNREGA can give people an opportunity to make the entire system truly transparent and accountable. Properly supported, people's struggles for basic entitlements can, in turn, become the strongest political initiatives to strengthen our democratic fabric.

Table 1.1: Milestones of the Indian Journey towards MGNREGA (1952-2009)

Year	Programmes/Schemes
1952	Community Development Programme (CDP)
1971-72	Crash Scheme for Rural employment (CRSE)
1972	Pilot Intensive Rural Employment Programme (PIREP)
1973-76	Marginal Farmers and Agricultural Labour Scheme (MFAL), Drought-prone Area Programme (DPAP)
1974	Small Farmers Development Agency (SFDA)
1975	Twenty-Point Programme (TPP)
1977	Food for Work Programme (FWP) and Antyodaya Programme
1979	Training Rural Youth for Self-Employment (TRYSEM)
1980	National Rural Employment Programme (NREP), Integrated Rural Development Programme (IRDP)
1983	Rural Landless Employment Guarantee Programme (RLEGP), Development of Women and Children in Rural Areas (DWCRA)
1989-94	Jawahar Rozgar Yojana (JRY), Employment Assurance Scheme (EAS), Prime Ministers Rozgar Yojana (PMRY), Nehru Rozgar Yojana (NRY)
1999-2000	Swarnajayanthi Gram Swarozgar Yojana (SGSY), Antyodaya Anna Yojana (AAY), Pradan Manthri Gram Sadak Yojana (PMGSY)
2001	Sampoorna Grameen Rozgar Yojana (SGRY)
2006	NREGA introduced in 200 districts
2007	NREGA Phase II- Extended to additional 130 Districts.
2008	NREGA Phase III-Extended to cover all districts of India
2009	NREGA renamed as Mahatma Gandhi National Rural Employment Guarantee Act (MGNREGA)

Independent India has to acknowledge the critical role, MGNREGA has played in providing a measure of inclusive growth. It has given the people a right to work, to re-establish the dignity of labour, to ensure people's economic and democratic rights and entitlements, to create labour intensive infrastructure and asset, and to build the human resource base of the country. Thus, the Act gives hope to those who had all but lost their hope. It has a clear focus on the poorest of poor. It seeks to reach out to those in need of livelihood security. It gives employment, income, livelihood, and a chance to live a life of self-respect and dignity. The government has referred to it as, *"an Act of the people, by the people and for the people"*.

1.3 Employment Generation through MGNREGA

MGNREGA focuses on the districts having high incidence of poverty. However, it goes beyond poverty reduction and recognizes employment as a legal right. Sceptics considered it as a populist measure while others have considered it as a landmark initiative towards poverty alleviation and empowerment of the poor.

It is argued that this would not only increase the incomes of the poor, but the asset creation through the process of employment would generate a much needed productive infrastructure for poverty alleviation on a permanent basis.

There has been a "significant dent" in poverty in rural areas as the implementation of MGNREGA has increased earnings of rural households resulting in an increase in their purchasing power. With the increase in employment opportunities and wage rates (under NREGA), there has been a significant dent in poverty reduction in rural areas. Initially, the programme was implemented in 200 backward districts, identified by the Planning Commission. This posed a major challenge towards the implementation of the MGNREGA because of the special problems of the above areas. They are the least developed areas of the country comprising mostly marginal farmers and forest dwellers. It was implemented in a various phases. In phase one, it was implemented in 200 backward districts of the country, an additional 130 districts were added in phase two in 2007-08 and remaining 266 districts were notified in September 2008 and as on date, the scheme has been extended to all the districts of the country. In many of these districts, poverty has increased despite consistent focus of several poverty eradication programmes.

Governance has little or no presence in most of these districts.

One of the most important aspects of MGNREGA is that the villagers can rightfully demand employment. The authority is responsible for providing employment in response to demand or providing employment allowance otherwise. For performance analysis, it is essential to look at the response of government in providing employment against the demand raised by workers. MGNREGA can target development using huge demand for casual jobs. It has made a dent on poverty by increasing employment opportunities (Table 1.2).

Table 1.2: Employment Scenario in India under MGNREGA

Year	No. of HHs Registered	Employment Demanded by HH	Employment Provided to HH	Employment Provided (percent)
2006-07	37850390	21188894	21016099	99.18
2007-08	64740595	34326563	33909132	98.78
2008-09	100145950	45518907	45115358	99.12
2009-10	112548976	52920154	52585999	99.37
2010-11	120095282	54008043	53384234	98.84
2011-12	118595083	31724531	31105136	98.04
2012-13	135478282	50101754	48251564	96.30
2013-14	136578935	51765569	47684864	92.11
2014-15*	138953563	35809916	28619099	79.91

*as on 31.08.2014; Note: HH: Household

Source: www.nrega.nic.in

However, there have been inter-state variations in executing the scheme. Certain states have performed well in terms of employment provided as against employment demanded. The all-India level data shows that the country is able to provide employment to 99 percent of households as against their demand across the years, but of late, it has shown a declining trend. If we look at the state-wise analysis, the state of Andhra Pradesh performed well, as it was able to provide 100 percent employment continuously under the scheme followed by Tamil Nadu, Rajasthan, Gujarat, Maharashtra, Madhya Pradesh etc.; with low performance by Himachal Pradesh which can be perceived from Table 1.3.

Thus, if we take the percentage of households who demanded for employment and actual employment generated at national level, it seems to be around 99 percent with minor variation in different financial years, meaning that government was able to produce employment opportunities for those who demanded employment. Several factors explain the reasons for varying degrees of progress across states and even across districts within a state.

Table 1.3: Employment Provided as against Employment Demanded under MGNREGA

(in percent)

States	2006-07	2007-08	2008-09	2009-10	2012-13	2013-14	2014-15*
Andhra Pradesh	99.99	100	100	100	100	89.76	82.71
Assam	99.26	96.87	87.1	99.91	99.51	95.45	73.66
Bihar	98.84	97.08	100	100	97.71	85.66	64.48
Gujarat	100	100	100	100	98.45	89.97	79.87
Haryana	100	100	94.84	100	99.51	89.25	64.52
Himachal Pradesh	94.53	98.42	98.23	99.63	89.68	94.19	76.01
Karnataka	99.39	99.28	98.86	97.49	99.7	75.93	52.36
Madhya Pradesh	104.8	100	100	99.99	97.88	91.80	83.65
Maha-rashtra	109.0	100	99.84	99.99	99.07	90.39	84.59
Punjab	99.56	100	100	99.72	99.43	90.55	70.95
Rajasthan	100	99.88	99.97	100	99.18	91.56	86.23
Odisha	99.07	96.67	98.23	98.71	99.48	90.43	77.11
West Bengal	95.31	98.04	100	99.73	98.59	95.06	72.14
Uttar Pradesh	96.15	99.81	99.95	96.75	99.64	90.29	62.55
Tamil Nadu	99.96	100	100	100	99.31	99.41	99.38
Kerala	94.10	96.63	99.04	99.84	99.90	90.76	62.63
India	**99.18**	**98.78**	**99.11**	**99.36**	**98.93**	**92.11**	**79.91**

*as on 31.08.2014

Source: www.nrega.nic.in

Strong political will, presence of civil society agencies and NGOs, higher levels of awareness among the communities, and prior experience and capacities of civil servants and officials with regard to implementing similar programmes (like drought relief schemes) were identified as some of the factors responsible for a better take-off of MGNREGA in states like Andhra Pradesh, Tamil Nadu and Rajasthan.

1.4 Wages Rate under MGNREGA

Casual wage labourers are one of the most disadvantaged groups in the labour market. While their work contract is terminated and renewed on a daily basis, poor working conditions and low wages push them below poverty line. In 2004-05, average casual wage for males and females was ₹ 55 and ₹ 35 respectively in rural areas and ₹ 75 and ₹ 44 respectively in urban areas. On an average, in 2004-05, casual workers received far less wages than what was received by regular workers. In addition to low wages for casual workers, there is also gender bias in wage payments. It is important to note that the gender bias in casual wage payment is low in rural areas (0.63) than in urban areas (0.58). However, the reason for low gender bias in wage payments in rural areas was the highly suppressed wages both for male and female rural workers. The gender bias was also noticeable in case of urban regular workers.

MGNREGA provides provision for equal wages for men and women [Schedule II (34)] without any discrimination. The minimum wage of ₹ 100 a day under MGNREGA had increased the wage level across the private sector, benefiting both the families that could not avail MGNREGA work and families that had completed MGNREGA quota of 100 days work. It provided the poor with required support in the labour market by not letting them below a certain level. It has increased the bargaining power of the poor people in the labour market. The workers of MGNREGA, earlier, were mostly voiceless and they could not normally bargain for higher wages. Now, wages under MGNREGA have become a benchmark and MGNREGA workers bargain for wages and are no longer willing to work for lesser wages. The scheme has improved the lives of the people and has brought stability and assured incomes to the families that were until recently desperately poor (Vidya Subramanian, 2009). A study conducted by the Institute of Applied Manpower Research covering a sample of 6,000 households across 20 states in the country (300 samples per state) has revealed that the low earning level of a number of beneficiaries declined and the number of households reporting marginally higher income has increased (K. Balchand, 2009).

In certain places, especially during the lean season, MGNREGA had been the only source of income (Sudha Narayan, 2008). This upward pressure on rural wages has given rise to two distinct trends. One, workers are finding it better to stay back instead of migrating because of better incomes at home. In most of the states, the incidence of out-migration was extremely high prior to the implementation of MGNREGA. At least one member from each household had migrated to different places like Punjab and Haryana for manual work.

With the commencement of MGNREGA, employment had been ensured in the native place resulting in lowering of out-migration. The income earned through MGNREGA works and the savings accumulated by working as migrant labourers in faraway places was invested for increasing the paddy yield. Further, the impetus for improving the crop yield came from the fact that they now have to depend on crop cultivation more than when they were migrating out.

The participation in this programme is expected to contribute to higher consumption and asset accumulation of direct beneficiaries through three channels. First, it directly transfers financial resources to the participating households and enhances the household income, which would consequently increase the total consumption and nutritional intake. Second, increased income encourages poor households to save and invest, which could eventually help the poor to be involved in diverse productive activities. Third, most of time work takes the form of irrigation and land development and the work sites are often in participants' own fields. Resultantly, the participants may be paid for increasing the productivity of their own land—increased productivity may lead to higher income and consumption.

The additional income has transformed the composition of the food consumption pattern. Very poor families are also able to supplement nutritional items like vegetables and pulses and are having a more balanced diet. The evidences are illustrative and over a period of time, if there is a reduction in the malnourishment of children in MGNREGA Panchayats, the impact of additional income will be sufficiently substantiated. There is a clear tendency of using the additional wage income for the education of children. It builds a case of inherent demand for children's better education. Most of the MGNREGA benefited families' utilized their income for accessing children's education or supplementing with additional facilities to improve the quality of education. This long-term investment of MGNREGA wage earners would enhance the capacity of the families for their upward mobility. A number of studies carried out in recent years have shown that the MGNREGA has had a significant positive impact on rural wages.

1.5 Employment to SCs and STs

In India, important social groups such as scheduled castes and scheduled tribes which are at the lowest rung of the social and economic hierarchy together constitute about 23 percent of the total population. However, their shares in the development outcomes are far too low in terms of resource endowments as well as human development indicators. Their presence is disproportionately high in groups such as agriculture labour households, small and marginal farmers as well as unorganized workers. Poverty and vulnerability is also high among these groups compared to other social groups. Given this situation, MGNREGA appeared to be a critical source of employment for the rural poor, particularly for categories such as distressed families from SCs and STs (Table 1.4).

The data suggests that as a measure of social protection to the poor and vulnerable social groups, the scheme is making a difference by augmenting their employment and incomes. In all states, the share of SCs and STs in the employment generated under the scheme is much higher than their share in population.

Table 1.4: Employment of SCs under MGNREGA

Year	Total	SCs	Percent
2006-07	9050.54	2295.23	25.36
2007-08	14367.95	3942.34	27.43
2008-09	21632.86	6336.18	29.28
2009-10	28359.57	8644.83	30.48
2010-11	25715.23	7875.63	30.62
2011-12	14367.95	3942.34	27.43
2012-13	21848.00	4726.75	21.63
2013-14	21867.70	4941.37	22.60
2014-15*	8540.51	1938.81	22.70

*as on 31.08.2014

Source: www.nrega.nic.in

Even in Gujarat and Rajasthan, where it was lower initially, there has been a substantial increase in the later years. Concentration of SC and ST population varies in different states. Hence, figures of SC/ST workdays generated can be meaningfully interpreted with the availability of percentage of SC/ST population in the MGNREGA districts. However, the following trend emerged from the person days generated. At the national level, the participation of SCs showed an increasing trend from 25.36 percent in 2006-07 to 30.62 percent in 2010-11, but subsequently declined to 22.60 percent in 2013-14, with wider variation across the states (Table 1.5).

Thus, MGNREGA provided a solution for inclusive growth by providing legal guarantee to employment for the under privileged sections of the society in the country.

Tables 1.6 and 1.7 show the participation of STs under

MGNREGA.

1.6 Participation of Women under MGNREGA

The National Rural Employment Guarantee Act is an epoch making event in the history of independent India. There is much that the MGNREGA promises from the perspective of women's empowerment as well. Most boldly, in a rural milieu marked by stark inequalities between men and women—in the opportunities for gainful employment afforded as well as wage rates—MGNREGA represents action on both these counts.

Table 1.5: Participation of SCs in Major States under MGNREGA

(in percent)

States	2006-07	2007-08	2008-09	2009-10	2012-13	2013-14	2014-15*
Andhra Pradesh	29.82	27.72	26.14	24.67	23.99	23.23	23.51
Assam	8.652	7.6	10.41	12.14	5.78	6.46	7.2
Bihar	47.08	45.66	50.07	45.30	23.97	28.36	28.19
Gujarat	7.036	5.918	12.67	14.87	8.99	7.61	7.42
Haryana	60.03	53.8	53.03	53.58	52.27	48.41	45.39
Himachal Pradesh	30.4	32.31	33.52	33.35	23.32	28.44	27.55
Karnataka	33.05	30.23	27.77	16.70	16.95	15.89	15.16
Madhya Pradesh	15.87	17.87	17.82	18.48	19.19	18.51	16.48
Maha-rashtra	16.19	18.44	16.51	25.61	16.93	9.58	9.63
Punjab	69.36	76.29	74.22	78.92	78.27	76.94	77.60
Rajasthan	15.97	19.24	28.79	26.53	18.38	19.84	18.77
Odisha	23.65	24.33	20.24	19.16	18.11	16.36	16.67
West Bengal	36.08	36.28	37.45	36.85	32.95	32.98	34.10
Uttar Pradesh	56.85	53.75	53.56	56.41	33.75	33.14	32.11
Tamil Nadu	56.06	57.36	60.27	59.07	28.19	29.58	20.09
Kerala	20.1	14.76	19.47	16.77	15.26	15.65	19.81
India	**25.36**	**27.44**	**29.29**	**30.48**	**22.05**	**22.60**	**22.70**

*as on 31.08.2014

Source: www.nrega.nic.in

The Act stipulates that wages will be equal for men and

women. It is also committed to ensuring that at least 33 percent of the workers shall be women.

Table 1.6: Employment of STs under MGNREGA

Year	Total	STs	Percent
2006-07	9050.54	3298.73	36.44
2007-08	14367.95	4205.60	29.27
2008-09	21632.86	5501.64	25.43
2009-10	28359.57	5874.39	20.71
2010-11	25715.23	5361.79	20.85
2011-12	14367.95	4205.60	29.27
2012-13	21848.00	3627.81	16.60
2013-14	21867.70	3758.22	17.19
2014-15*	8540.51	1404.72	16.45

*as on 31.08.2014

Source: www.nrega.nic.in

By generating employment for women at fair wages in the village, MGNREGA can play a substantial role in economically empowering women and laying the basis for greater independence and self-esteem. However, provisions like priority for women in the ratio of one-third of total workers [Schedule II (6)]; equal wages for men and women [Schedule II (34)]; and crèches for the children of women workers [Schedule II (28)] were made in the Act, with the view to ensuring that rural women benefit from the scheme in a certain manner.

Provisions like work within a radius of five kilometres from the house, absence of supervisor and contractor, and flexibility in terms of choosing period and months of employment were not made exclusively for women, but have, nevertheless, been conducive for rural women. Nevertheless, women have availed of the paid employment opportunity under MGNREGA in large numbers.

Implementation of MGNREGA has contributed to very high levels of women empowerment, particularly in the following aspects—that as the work is organized by women's groups, the gender perspective gets built in automatically—for the first time equal wages are really paid and this has boosted the earnings of women.

Table 1.7: Participation of STs in Major States under MGNREGA

(in percent)

States	2006-07	2007-08	2008-09	2009-10	2012-13	2013-14	2014-15*
Andhra Pradesh	13.01	12.79	12.95	14.71	15.38	14.56	10.8
Assam	46.26	39.12	34.45	31.02	20.46	16.09	10.72
Bihar	3.205	2.458	2.655	2.163	1.87	2.11	1.77
Gujarat	64.26	65.92	50.56	39.46	37.52	41.05	40.17
Haryana	0	0	0	0	0.04	0	0
H.P	22.40	11.03	7.789	8.7	7.06	7.37	7.63
Karnataka	20.35	19.18	13.87	8.575	27.66	7.93	8.23
Madhya Pradesh	48.63	48.76	46.81	45.34	9.20	29.82	28.4
Maharashtra	40.88	38.49	44.17	33.16	14.37	18.93	16.61
Punjab	0.00	0.00	0.00	0.00	0.04	0.04	0
Rajasthan	64.36	46.39	23.24	22.5	24.09	26.16	30.08
Odisha	49.27	39.65	35.81	36.26	37.10	40.82	37.4
West Bengal	18.60	13.8	14.81	14.38	9.55	9.45	9.04
Uttar Pradesh	3.113	1.84	1.962	1.482	1.05	0.99	0.66
Tamil Nadu	2.374	2.63	1.739	2.495	1.31	1.28	1.03
Kerala	12.39	13.03	9.26	5.33	2.59	2.67	5.56
India	**36.44**	**29.27**	**25.43**	**20.71**	**16.73**	**17.19**	**16.45**

*as on 31.08.2014

Source: www.nrega.nic.in

It can also help to empower women, by giving them independent income-earning opportunities. As bank deposits are increasing, the intra-household status of the women has also been improving commensurately as she now controls substantial cash resources and withdrawal can be made only by her consent. There are wide variations across states, within states and across districts in the share of work days going to women (Table 1.8).

Participation of women has increased significantly. In several states, participation of women has surpassed men's participation.

Table 1.8: Employment of Women under MGNREGA

Year	Total	Women	Percent
2006-07	9050.54	3679.0	40.64
2007-08	14368.0	6109.1	42.51
2008-09	21632.9	10357.3	47.87
2009-10	28359.6	13640.5	48.09
2010-11	25715.2	12274.2	47.73
2011-12	14367.9	6109.12	42.51
2012-13	21848.0	11388.5	52.13
2013-14	21867.7	11554.6	52.84
2014-15*	8540.5	4937.6	57.81

*as on 31.08.2014
Source: www.nrega.nic.in

There are various explanations for the varying participation of women workers under the MGNREGA. Factors that have encouraged women workers' participation include the nature of the job not requiring special knowledge and skill; out-migration of male family members; the employment opportunity being available at the doorstep; a tradition of rural women working in others' fields; the provision of equal, non-discriminatory wages; and innovative experiments in implementation like the female mate system in Rajasthan, synergisation of MGNREGA with Kudumbashree in Kerala, and in Bihar, gender differential tasks for uniform (minimum) wages (Table 1.9).

1.7 Financial Performance and Inclusion

The finance forms the most critical input for every programme implementation in order to grow and survive. Government of India releases the funds through budgetary policies for programme implementation and it has shown a steady increase over the years (Table 1.10).

Table 1.9: Women Participation of Major States under MGNREGA-National Scenario

(in percent)

States	2006-07	2007-08	2008-09	2009-10	2012-13	2013-14	2014-15*
Andhra Pradesh	54.79	57.74	58.15	58.17	58.07	58.71	58.87
Assam	31.67	30.85	27.16	27.76	25.72	24.75	23.39
Bihar	17.38	26.61	30.02	30.04	30.41	34.94	37.47
Gujarat	50.20	46.54	42.82	47.55	42.68	43.97	43.88
Haryana	30.56	34.42	30.64	34.81	39.85	41.7	41.97
H.P	12.24	30.10	39.01	46.09	61.06	62.52	58.79
Karna-taka	50.56	50.26	50.42	36.79	46.33	46.59	46.66
Madhya Pradesh	43.24	41.67	43.27	44.22	42.47	42.64	43.92
Maha-rashtra	37.07	39.99	46.22	39.65	44.51	43.7	45.85
Punjab	37.76	16.29	24.60	26.28	46.33	52.74	58.38
Rajas-than	67.14	68.99	67.10	66.89	69.14	67.76	69.07
Odisha	35.64	36.39	37.58	36.25	36.39	33.57	34.33
West Bengal	18.28	16.99	26.52	33.42	33.21	35.45	38.76
Uttar Pradesh	16.55	14.52	18.10	21.67	19.39	22.17	25.31
Tamil Nadu	81.11	82.00	79.66	82.91	74.84	84.04	85.56
Kerala	64.31	72.55	85.01	88.19	92.95	93.37	94.12
India	**40.65**	**42.51**	**47.87**	**48.19**	**52.44**	**52.84**	**57.81**

*as on 31.08.2014

Source: www.nrega.nic.in

Access to finance for those belonging to poor and vulnerable groups is a pre-requisite for poverty reduction and social cohesion. It has to become an integral part of our efforts to promote inclusive growth.

In fact, providing access to finance is a form of empowerment of the vulnerable groups. Financial inclusion is a process of ensuring delivery of financial services to vulnerable groups which is timely, adequate and at an affordable cost. The various financial services include credit, savings, insurance and payments and remittance facilities.

Table 1.10: Financial Allocation of MGNREGA Funds

Years	Budget Allocation (₹ crore)	Percent of Expenditure on Wages	Percent of Expenditure on Material	Percent of Administ-rative Expenditure
2006-07	11,300	66.21	30.89	2.09
2007-08	12,000	68.54	30.58	3.12
2008-09	30,000	69.27	30.8	3.48
2009-10	39,100	69.77	30.23	3.29
2010-11	40,100	68.36	31.64	4.57
2011-12	40,000	76.39	23.61	3.69
2012-13	33,000	75.30	24.71	4.56
2013-14	33,000	72.97	27.03	4.72
2014-15	34,000	80.43	19.57	2.97

Source: www.nrega.nic.in

MGNREGA has been revolutionary in its promise of inclusive growth and financial inclusion, the right to work and the dignity of labour and a rational, participatory relationship with the state.

With a view to infuse transparency and enhancing the integrity of wage payment under MGNREGA, and also to encourage savings among the rural poor, Schedule II of MGNREGA Act has been amended to make wage disbursement to MGNREGA workers through institutional accounts in banks or post offices.

Wage payments through MGNREGA have initiated the biggest "financial inclusion" drive, with the requirement that all wage payments be made through banks and post offices. Payment of wages to workers employed under MGNREGA works can be done with speed, reliability, low transaction costs and leakages, if each worker has a bank account in which wages are transferred periodically.

Now with the implementation of MGNREGA, large flow of funds is occurring from government to the rural households, which has opened a new chapter in the history of rural development in India. The wage payments through banks and post offices had been a step forward in many ways, notably by enabling millions of people to open bank or post office accounts and by making it much hard for corrupt middlemen to embezzle wage funds. It separates the implementing agency from the payment agency. Hence, as against direct payment of cash to the labourers by the panchayat/block authorities (or even contractors), who could keep a share of the money for themselves, in the banking system the money goes directly into the account of the labourers.

This would also discourage corrupt authorities from fudging the muster rolls. Moreover, the payment through banks and post offices would promote the habit of savings among rural unskilled workers.

Under the new system of financial inclusion, 10.02 crore MGNREGA workers accounts were opened and about 90 percent of wages were disbursed through these accounts up to August 2014—accounting for 75 percent of the expenditure under the programme. Such huge flow of funds from government treasury to the poor rural households provides an immense opportunity to bring the beneficiaries into the fold of the organized banking system. Although this new system has been hailed as a foolproof, cost-effective solution to reduce leakages and to promote greater transparency, the transition was rushed and several complications with the new system are now becoming apparent. As per 2013-14 data, there were more than thousand banks working in different parts of country with 10.02 crore of accounts for MGNREGA workers, the largest financial inclusion scheme of the rural poor by which wages are being disbursed through these accounts. These accounts have also encouraged thrift and saving among some of the poorest families.

1.7.1 Benefits of Bank Payment:

1. Reduced cost of payment delivery for the government if new accounts are opened for recipients or alternative payment channels used.
2. Recipients need not go out of their way to receive payments.

3. Payments delivered more quickly.
4. Reduction in number of fictitious or duplicate beneficiaries.
5. Reduction in cases of fraud where funds are siphoned off without recipients' awareness—for one it separates the implementing agency from the payment agency.
6. Avoidance of middlemen or agents for transaction.
7. Relationship with financial system.
8. Social recognition.
9. Access to financial products for economic growth and well-being.

1.8 Creating Community Assets under MGNREGA

The prime object of MGNREGA is to provide guaranteed wage employment to rural poor by creating community assets. At the grassroot, these community assets fulfil the basic amenities of the local populace and bridge the gap of general amenities. The Act attempts to unlock the potential of the rural poor to contribute to the reconstruction of their environment. To achieve this, it has laid emphasis on creation of productive assets in villages. Out of nine preferred areas of works under the MGNREGA, seven focus on water and soil conservation. As per Schedule 1 of the Act, the focus of the MGNREGA shall be on the following works:

1. Water conservation and water harvesting;
2. Drought proofing, including afforestation and tree plantation;
3. Irrigation canals, including micro and minor irrigation works;
4. Provision of irrigation facility to land owned by households belonging to the SC/ST, or to land of the beneficiaries of land reforms, or to land of the beneficiaries under the Indira Awas Yojana;
5. Renovation of traditional water bodies, including de-silting of tanks;
6. Land development;

7. Flood control and protection works, including drainage in waterlogged areas;
8. Rural connectivity to provide all-weather access. The construction of roads may include culverts where necessary, and within the village area may be taken up along with drains;
9. Any work that may be notified by the central government in consultation with the state government. In terms of implementation priority, the programme mandates that maximum emphasis should be on water conservation.

The MGNREGA is probably the world's largest ecological security programme, with the key provision that investments in an employment guarantee programme must be in productive and eco-friendly assets. This would ensure that the resultant growth dynamic is both sustainable (by regenerating the environment) and non-inflationary (by easing the agrarian constraint). Not only does demand need stimulation, growth has to be sustainable in both economic and ecological terms, especially in these times of climate change. For the nine years so far, during which MGNREGA has been operational, the purpose of the Act was to create rural assets, important among them being water and soil conservation projects, especially minor irrigation works. Table 1.11 shows various types of work undertaken through MGNREGA from 2006-07 to 2014-15.

The national scenario shows that highest work has been completed under the provision of water conservation and harvesting which accounted for an average of 23.28 percent of total work completed in the country followed by the rural connectivity with an average of 20.26 percent, land development with 14.04 percent and micro irrigation at 6.17 percent, with wide variation across states and across the years.

The MGNREGA addresses itself chiefly to working people and their fundamental right to live with dignity. The success of the MGNREGA, however, will depend on people's realization of the Act as a right. Effective levels of awareness and sustained public pressure are crucial to ensure that the implementation problems are addressed to and the objectives met.

Table 1.11: Asset Creation under MGNREGA in India

(in percent)

Items	2006-07	2007-08	2008-09	2009-10	2012-13	2013-14	2014-15
Rural Connectivity	23.64	20.58	18.54	15.71	20.72	20.78	12.86
Flood control and Protection	2.814	10.23	5.152	4.24	4.032	3.57	1.79
Water Conservation and harvesting	31.8	24.03	20.44	27.87	22.56	11.29	8.96
Drought Proofing	8.058	6.956	6.214	5.12	7.841	11.49	4.32
Micro Irrigation	3.213	5.621	5.45	6.71	8.146	4.29	2.01
Provision of Irrigation Facility	7.094	6.628	19.61	15.97	10.9	23.67	12.26
Renovation of traditional Water bodies	6.696	10.42	7.62	7.2	8.414	3.48	4.32
Land Development	11.32	11.15	15.61	15.15	12.96	7.50	10.61
Any other activity approved by MRD	5.367	4.385	1.37	1.99	2.717	6.20	1.76

Source: www.nrega.nic.in

The nine year programme implementation has made much effect on rural people by creating adequate employment through creating community assets with active participation of people, especially the vulnerable sections of society like SCs, STs and women through mobilization and flow of huge financial resources.

Without development of rural community it becomes difficult for development of the state. MGNREGA should aim for an India in which the poorest shall feel that it is their country in whose making they have an effective voice, an India in which there shall be no high class and low class of people, an India in which all communities shall live in perfect harmony. It is important to note that the Act is still in its infancy and it may take years to put in place the tools and instruments needed to actualise the right to employment through a scheme, even in the best of circumstances.

References

Balchand.K (2009), "NREGA Lifts up Standard of Living", *The Hindu*, September 6, p. 18.

Basu, A.K. (2011), "Impact Of Rural Employment Guarantee Schemes on Seasonal Labour Markets: Optimum Compensation and Workers' Welfare", IZA Discussion Paper No. 5701, College of William and Mary, ZEF, University of Bonn and IZA.

Basu, K. (1981), "Food for Work Programmes: Beyond Roads That Get Washed Away", *Economic and Political Weekly*, 16: 37-40.

Bhatty, Kiran (2006), "Employment Guarantee and Child Rights", *Economic and Political Weekly*, 41(20): 1965-1967.

Drèze, J. and A. Sen (1991), "Strategies of Entitlement Protection", *Hunger and Public Action.* 1: 104-122.

Dreze, Jean (2007), "Employment a Social Responsibility", *The Hindu*, November 22.

Dreze, Jean (2009), "Making NREGA Work", *G.B. Pant Social Science Institute*, Allahabad University.

IHD (2008), "Processes, Institutions and Mechanisms of Implementation of NREGA: Impact Assessment of Bihar and Jharkhand", *Institute for Human Development*, New Delhi.

IHD (2009b), "Women's Empowerment through Guaranteed Employment: A Case Study of NREGA Implementation in Bihar, Jharkhand, Rajasthan and Himachal Pradesh", New Delhi.

IHD (2009c), "Institutional and Governance Challenges in Social Protection: Designing Implementation Models for the Right to Work Programme in India", Working Paper submitted under the Social Protection in Asia Programme.

Kannan, K.P. (2005), "Linking Employment Guarantee to Human

Development", *Economic and Political Weekly*, October 15.

Khera, Reetika and Nandini Nayak (2009), "Women Workers and Perceptions of the National Rural Employment Guarantee Act", *Economic and Political Weekly,* 44(43): 49-57.

Khera, Reetika (2008), "Empowerment Guarantee Act", *Economic and Political Weekly,* 43(35): 8-10.

Krishnaraj, Maithreyi, Divya Pandey and Aruna Kanchi (2004), "Does EGS Require Restructuring for Poverty Alleviation and Gender Equality?: Gender Concerns and Issues for Restructuring", *Economic and Political Weekly,* 39(17): 174-177.

Mehrotra, Santosh (2008), "NREGA Two Years On: Where Do We Go from Here?", *Economic and Political Weekly,* 43(31): 27-35.

National Rural Employment Guarantee Act (2005), "Operational Guidelines (2005)", *Ministry of Rural Development, Government of India,* New Delhi.

Pankaj, Ashok and Rukmini Tankha (2009), "Women's Empowerment through Guaranteed Employment: A Case Study of NREGA Implementation in Bihar, Jharkhand, Rajasthan and Himachal Pradesh", Report for UNIFEM, *Institute for Human Development,* New Delhi.

Rania, Antonopoulos, (2009), "The Right to a Job, The Right Types of Projects: Employment Guarantee Policies from a Gender Perspective", *Economists for Full Employment.*

Ravallion, M. (1999), "Appraising Workfare", *World Bank Research Observer*, 14: 31-48.

Sengupta, Arjun (2007), "NREGA is one of the Most Successful Programmes for Poverty Alleviation: *The Hindu,* September 5.

Talukdar, Ratna Bharali (2008), "NREGA Shines for Tripura Women", *India Together*, June 30.

Vijayamohanan, N. Pillai (2010), "Mid Term Appraisal of the XI Plan of Kerala Study II Performance of 15 Major Centrally Sponsored Flagship Programmes", Centre for Development Studies (CDS), Trivandrum, Kerala.

Vijayanand, S.M. and V.N. Jitherdran (2009), "Implementation of NREGA Experience of Kerala" in *NREGA: Design Process and Impact*, *UNDP,* New Delhi, p. 220.

2

Employment Multiplier-Accelerator Interaction in MGNREGA

2.1 Great Depression and Keynesian Economics

Until roughly the Great Depression of the 1930s, the right of the individual to employment under capitalism was considered entirely in the context of a market economy. But the Great Depression and the devastation caused by the World Wars gave way to a different problem amongst the advanced capitalist countries of the world. The market left on its own, could not keep the show going without the active intervention of the state. In the United States, after several attempts to promote market forces, and a disbelief in Keynes' recommendations for increased government spending to boost aggregate demand, policymakers came to realize that *laissez faire* economics was not the solution to the problem at hand and that the government had to act as an employer of the last resort. Keynes argued, "The government should pay people to dig holes in the ground and then fill them up, it doesn't matter what they do as long as the government is creating jobs".

Ideas that the state needs to act in mitigating unemployment to put capitalism back on track became attractive and Keynes' theory was accepted more easily in that situation. Keynes' economic policy was interventionist, arguing that governments should create jobs for the unemployed to increase their spending power, create a class of consumers and thus stimulate the economy through the labour intensive techniques of the economy. However, the extent to which these labour intensive public works programmes can have an impact on growth and equity, beyond simply being a last resort fall back coping option for poor households, depends on a number of issues. These include the planning of the programmes, the wage rate, the nature of work and thereby the types of jobs being generated and the access and availability of work for women and men. While the problem of economic instability and depressed effective demand is central across regions subject to capitalist production, we need a consideration of the consequence of adopting any blanket macroeconomic policy that assumes a desire to preserve (or enhance) these very capitalist relations.

According to Keynes, government could reverse economic downturns by borrowing money from the private sector and then returning the money to the private sector through various spending programmes. He also encouraged budget deficits on the ground that these would boost growth by injecting purchasing power into the economy. MGNREGA can be taken akin to the interventionist policy as prescribed during the Great Depression in US by Keynes. These programmes are based on a Keynesian aggregate demand strategy of direct job creation by the government for a full employment economy. These are usually, targeted jobs programmes, paying minimum wages, with an aim to create a social floor, productive assets and have the potential to reduce poverty 'in a politically digestible manner'.

This 'employment of last resort' programme based on government expenditure would be stabilizing and stimulating for the economy by generating guaranteed employment. The rationale for these programmes are based on the premise that the government has an active role to play in promoting full employment in developing economies by assuming the role of the market maker for labour. An exploration on whether the MGNREGA has been able to fulfil its role of being the Indian version of the Keynesian scheme, like other schemes, brings about a lot of discussion on whether one should see it in the light of merely being an employment generation programme or one should perceive it as one which will impact the labour market drastically, providing an opportunity for labourers to not only demand for work but also demand for their rights as a collective unit, under the banner of being a worker and not an individual carrying social and political identity tags attached with their names. This programme involves the establishment of a federally funded but locally decentralized job-creation programme—a rural works programme which secures an infinitely elastic demand for labour, ensuring simultaneously full employment and price stability.

What Indian policy has recognized is that such Keynesian style expenditures on public works can be important normally, even in the absence of price or income shocks, so as to smoothen and sustain seasonal fluctuations in labour demand and, therefore, wage rates in rural areas, wherein rainfall patterns and insufficient irrigation preclude year-round crop cultivation. The deceleration in employment growth since reforms period was further reinforced by a sharp cut back in public spending on rural employment programs (Dev, 2002). In this context, the enactment of MGNREGA is appropriate and timely.

2.2 Multiplier and Accelerator Principles

The concepts of multiplier and accelerator borrowed from macroeconomic theory illuminate the enormous potential of MGNREGA and help set standards that it must be judged by. Let us define the employment multiplier as an agent of change/increase in employment due to increase in government spending in the scheme. MGNREGA is a large-scale public works programme which creates purchasing power among workers or working on MGNREGA sites results in additional money which creates demand for commodities. The production of these commodities, in turn, creates demand for capital, raw materials and workers. The extra income so generated causes further demand, which again provides a stimulus to production, employment and demand...and so on in a spiral. This demand stimulating process is called the multiplier. The value of this multiplier depends on the marginal propensity to consume (MPC) of those benefiting from government intervention.

The MPC is our extra spending out of the additional rupee we earn. Clearly, the higher the MPC, the greater the stimulus provided to demand. The great thing about MGNREGA from this point of view is that it is putting money into the hands of those whose MPC is the highest. Those on the margins of existence are more likely to spend than save of what they earn. Apparently, demand in the economy is being sustained by rural buying, which has received a boost from MGNREGA incomes. Most of the MGNREGA workers are poor and have less purchasing power, but after introduction of the scheme most of earned income is spent on consumption rather than saving i.e. for meeting day to day expenses, so that there exists a high propensity to consume. Whatever funds are allocated for MGNREGA by the government for financing the scheme automatically stipulates the economy through the process of multiplier and can subsequently create additional 'spin-off' employment opportunities in other sectors of the economy.

Now let us estimate the effect or value of this employment multiplier when the government finances the schemes either by increasing tax or borrowings or by printing of money. Firstly, the scheme can be financed by increasing tax on consumption. However, an increase in tax will potentially reduce demand elsewhere as it appropriates purchasing power. This implies that the multiplier effect of demand generated through the employment providing public works may be negated by the reduction of demand elsewhere due to taxing away of purchasing power. It is merely a redistribution of resources from one hand to another. Thus, for every person employed, there should be one person unemployed somewhere else. So, in this case, employment multiplier is one. But generally we are taxing progressively which falls heavily on the richer sections of the society which doesn't reduce demand as much as imposing tax regressively.

Hence, while taxing progressively, wealth or income would be transferred from haves to have-nots which will increase the welfare of the community. If MGNREGA wage is paid accordingly, there is no fear of inflation, which is just merely a transfer of purchasing power from one to another. Secondly, the government can also finance this scheme through borrowings. There are several ways the government can borrow the required funds. It can borrow from the banking system at a low rate of interest via the statutory liquidity ratio (SLR) funds or the government can print money in order to raise funds. Here, there is no taking away of purchasing power from any part of the economy. The expenditure on the scheme will generate multiplier effects. In this case, employment multiplier is greater than one, as employment created by the MGNREGA shall in fact lead to an increase in demand in rural areas which will further lead to creation of more employment opportunities. But here the problem of inflation may arise.

When the government increases its expenditure from G to G_1 in the form of higher budgetary allocation for financing MGNREGA as stated above, there is an increase in autonomous spending given by $Z = (C_{0+}I+G-C_1T) \rightarrow Z = (C_{0+}I+G_1-C_1T)$, which results in increase in income Y as well as output and demand. As there is an increase in autonomous spending, the demand curve shifts upward in the form of higher purchasing power and at the same time the level of income increases from Y_1 to Y_2 where the demand is Z_1 and increases to Z_2.

Since the demand is more, companies will have to produce more and therefore they will have to make enhance their investments, employ more labour and thus there is further increase in wages and demand. Now we can explain the effect of MGNREGA with the help of following IS-LM model.

As government spending increases over years for the purpose of financing MGNREGA, the farmers, the workers and the labourers would get higher wages, thereby reflecting the accelerator effect of MGNREGA. The investment also increases and together with the increase in government spending and the increase in consumption it would lead to the shift in the IS curve towards right.

According to a survey, a very high proportion of agricultural labour households in India actually own land. The percentage is around 50 in Rajasthan and Madhya Pradesh, 60 in Odisha and Uttar Pradesh and over 70 in Chhattisgarh and Jharkhand. When farmers and workers from these sections (which include producers) avail the facilities of MGNREGA, they invest whatever savings they make under this project in their lands. This in turn helps these farmers to rebuild the decimated productivity of their farms. Public investment in this project incentivizes private investment. Given the private saving, if there is an increase in the government deficit, the investment must go down. The crucial part of this statement is "given private saving". Considering the above example, we can say that "If the increase in private savings (because of investments) is more than the increase in spending by Government", then a fiscal expansion—an increase in spending, may actually increase the investment.

Thus, a mutually reinforcing relationship between investment and income is catalyzed by MGNREGA. First, investment generates demand and income through the multiplier. Then, income stimulates investment via the accelerator, giving rise to a spiralling cycle repeated in successive rounds. Although not usually deployed in such a context, the accelerator principle in macroeconomic theory describes the positive impact of growing incomes on private fixed investment. Rising incomes also improve capacity utilisation and happier expectations act as incentives for larger investments. Under MGNREGA, farmers have come back to their land they have abandoned—as output increases, in an atmosphere of renewed hope, it spurs further investment.

Converging MGNREGA with other programmes for rural livelihoods would carry this momentum forward in a positive upward spiral, which will enhance the growth process via downstream multiplier-accelerator effects. Effectively, a wage employment programme can thus be transformed into a source of sustainable livelihood generating self-employment. This would permit reduction in allocations for MGNREGA over time, not only because landed labourers get back to their own farms but also because of a general rise in demand for labour in the rural economy.

2.3 Public Spending, Stabilization and Effective Demand through MGNREGA

The buffer-stock nature of the policy mandates that funding must be federal, as the program expands. The financial and economic crisis has had at least one significant impact on the world of ideas: it has brought back to the forefront the recognition of the crucial role of government expenditure in stabilizing economies and averting or mitigating recessions. In such a situation, monetary policy typically has a little effect in reviving economies.

Hence, the clear requirement is of a fiscal policy for the government to maintain an expansionary fiscal stance that will pull the economy out of the downswing. In a modern economic theory, these claims have no application and should not influence the design of policy.

In a modern monetary economy, responsible governance requires a policy framework that maximises the inclusion and involvement of the citizens in the productive process, maintaining a minimum standard of living and providing security from job loss. Fiscal deficits in such a context are not only acceptable but even necessary and essential to ensure economic recovery (Ghosh, J., 2009). Government during recession can take various counter-cyclical policies to stimulate the deficiency in effective demand, like MGNREGA programme.

The public programme will add to the annual deficit and the national debt, but those levels are just accounting indications of the private sector's desire to net saving and do not represent financial burden on the government (Wray, 1998, 1989; Forstater, 1999; Rima, 2003). It is the function of the deficit/debt such as achieving full employment that matters, not their levels (Lerner, 1943). As Vickrey (1993) states, when notions of government budget balancing "...compel us to tolerate the wastage of human resources and all the concomitant social problems that unemployment provokes, we must look at the 'real' side of the coin". The functional finance principles allow us to view government deficits as tools (Todorova, 2007). Government deficits can be employed for any purpose; for example, the composition of deficits and state policy can be formulated in a way that reinforces patriarchal relations. Direct job creation in the form of public works may be necessary in order to attain and maintain full employment and price stability (Lerner, 1944).

Hence, the design of MGNREGA program is crucial. However, the decentralized planning aspect of MGNREGA gives avenues for gender informed inputs from local communities and organizations. Because MGNREGA ensures that deficit spending is at the correct level to achieve full employment, there is no risk of inflation. Moreover, because it is an anti-cyclical policy, macroeconomic stability is improved.

What was truly innovative in Keynes's work was the principle of effective demand, which he spoke of for public works (Marcuzzo, 2006 and Chick, 1983). Unemployment for Keynes, in all cases (regardless of the phase in the business cycle), was a result of deficient effective demand. When employment at the bottom level is guaranteed, businesses, and households' expectations would be more stable. Households would know that they won't end up being a part of the reserve army of unemployed labour if they are ready, able, and willing to work for pay. Furthermore, business enterprises would have more stable expectations of effective demand.

Thus, MGNREGA will stabilize economic activity at full employment. The program would be permanent—but its size will vary depending on the business cycle which is driven by corporate investment decisions. The creation of infinitely elastic demand for labour at a floor (living) wage that does not depend on profit expectations of financiers and business, and generally on pecuniary valuation is a different approach from the standard idea of subsidizing demand (Minsky, 1986). Thus, this scheme in fact facilitates socialization of investment as described by Keynes. Furthermore, for Keynes, the key measure of the desirability of public policies was their net employment-generation effect. Targeting demand via public works would be done irrespective of the stage of the business cycle; whether this targeting meant more public works or better distributed public works depended on the level of economic activity.

With 'employer of last resort, unemployed workers are employed and their spending has multiplier effects on the economy which boosts aggregate demand and facilitates their incorporation into the private sector labour market. It ensures that deficit spending is at the correct level to achieve full employment—there is no risk of inflation. Moreover, since it is an anti-cyclical policy, macroeconomic stability is improved. Public spending on employment schemes, health and education, not only generates more direct employment but also more indirect employment because those who are newly employed by this are more likely to consume a higher proportion of their incomes. Fiscal policy that provides more wage income directly to unskilled workers in rural areas is likely to be much more effective in increasing aggregate incomes than other forms of public spending, because of the higher value of the multiplier in such expenditure. And therefore, particularly in the current situation of global economic crisis and national economic slowdown, expenditure on the MGNREGS assumes great significance.

Thus, MGNREGA provision requires billions of rupees, which, in turn, are being met by deficit financing to a great extent and diversion of resources from other productive sectors. The theory here is that increase in government spending can bolster economic growth by putting money into people's pockets, which creates purchasing power among workers. The great thing about MGNREGA from this point of view is that it is putting money into the hands of those whose MPC is the highest. Those on the margins of existence are more likely to spend than save most of what they earn. It makes each other powerful and effective if the implementation of MGNREGA is styled in a genuinely democratic and decentralized manner. As a result, the institutional machinery at the grassroots level would be stabilized to address both short-term and long-term measures to eradicate poverty, facilitate rural development and promote social equity in consultation with the local people (Ghosh, Satpaty and Kapur, 2008).

2.4 Inflation and MGNREGA

During the last decades, many economists and policymakers have approached employment in terms of its assumed relationship to inflation. If one assumes that wages and employment are determined solely by the operation of supply and demand curves for labour, then the level of employment is seen as creating an upward or downward pressure on wages and, therefore, on prices and inflation. By quoting monetary economics "inflation is always and everywhere a monetary phenomenon that arise from more rapid expansion in the quantity of money than in output". Whether, the effect of implementation of MGNREGA can cause inflation or not? It will come to say yes, at least in short-run. There are two major reasons behind it. Firstly, MGNREGA can cause a rise in money wages across the country and with the assumption of higher marginal propensity to consumption of MGNREGA workers being close to one, demand for food and other items would increase considerably. With the given assumption of constant supply in short-run, it will increase the price level and lead to growing inflation and would have large cascading effects in the related sectors. With higher inflation, workers feel that their purchasing power has been same as before and demand more wages and the decentralized and democratic political system is forced to increase wages further. These wage price spirals continue, thereby leading to wage-push inflation in the economy.

Secondly, MGNREGA can create shortage of supply of farm labour by giving them higher wage rate. Increased wage rate has adversely affected the availability of labour in the agricultural sector of many states where wages were very low before the introduction of MGNREGS and this resulted in increase in market wage rates particularly in Punjab, Haryana, Andhra Pradesh, Bengal and UP. This caused supply-side bottlenecks as one is not able to find enough hands at the time of harvesting season, when there is a high demand for labour. This further leads to the rise in price level and thus inflation appears. This supply-side bottlenecks and increase in wage rates as a result of government spending can be analyzed by using the aggregate demand and aggregate supply model.

The economy is equilibrium at point E with intersection of demand AD and supply AS. Now suppose as a result of financing of MGNREGA the nominal money supply increases. At each price level, the real balance is higher, interest rate is lower, and hence the demand for output rises. The aggregate demand schedule shifts rightward, proportionately to AD_1. At the initial price level P, there is now excess demand for goods. The firm finds that their investment and inventories are running down and accordingly hire more labour and raise output until economy reaches to E_1, the short-run equilibrium point. Note that at E_1, both output and next period's price have risen. Thus, monetary expansion leads to increase in price and output in short-run. The rise in price is due to the increase in labour cost or wages, as production and employment rise. The hike in price discourages the consumers to consume more.

Hence, the consumers reduce their consumption. Thus, the demand for goods produced is less. This discourages the producers to produce more. Thus, the output is reduced with an increased price level. This can be done by shifting the aggregate supply schedule up to AS_1, reflecting increase in wages that have taken place as a result of financing of MGNREGA. With new aggregate supply curve AS_1, and with aggregate demand unchanged at higher level AD_1, the new equilibrium is at E_{11}. Comparing to E_1 and E_{11}, we note that the output has now fallen compared with that of first period and price has risen further. This increase in wages has been passed by firms as an upward shift in AS curve and results in increase in price which reduces the real balance, rise in interest rates and lower equilibrium income and spending. If this process continues and supply curve shifts further to AS_{111} and new equilibrium now is E_{111}, resulted output will be declining towards full-employment level and price will keep rising and inflation will continue. The increase in expected price level and reduction in the output continues till the point, where output is equal to the original level of output, and the price level has increased to an extent.

We can say that MGNREGA project may lead to an increase in the general price level. Already, we have seen a rise in the price level of general food items. The concept of Phillip curve is also explained through MGNREGA. If more employment is created through MGNREGA, then there is lesser unemployment which is associated with higher inflation rate, that is, there is trade-off between inflation and unemployment.

However, this phenomenon is in the short-run and in the long-run, there is no inflation, because in the long-run, assets created by MGNREGA activities such as construction of well, dams for irrigation purposes, levelling of roads, water conservation and harvesting purposes, rural infrastructure would help in increase in the supply of items and thus reduce inflation. Public rural employment programme will preserve and could even enhance the productivity of the "reserve pool" of guaranteed job holders, and could potentially provide valuable public services which will reduce social and environmental costs. As Minsky put it, "only an infinitely elastic demand for labour can guarantee full employment without setting off a wage-price spiral, and only government can create an infinitely elastic demand for labour" (Minsky,

1986). At the same time, as long as those holding a guaranteed job are available, when private sector demand increases, then such a program would not result in inflationary pressures or structural rigidities.

The decentralized character of this programme provides avenues to ensure that jobs could be selected by local community groups and non-profit organizations. Thus, MGNREGA is an example of policy with a macroeconomic significance and effects, but with a local participation and democratic process in terms of determining what will be the composition of the activities in the programme and the social benefits to the community at the local level. The real challenge is the effective implementation of MGNREGA to ensure that assets built under the programme are durable—freshly built roads should not get washed away after the following year's monsoon. In other words, the programme has to work better than Keynes' prescriptions about digging holes.

Equally important is the imperative to improve the quality of governance and reduction in corruption. If a new architecture of implementation is put in place here, we could see not only the multiplier but a productivity enhancing accelerator in action that will transform the livelihoods of millions of our poor people, in a manner that is sustainable in both economic and ecological terms.

References

Appelbaum, Eileen (1978), "The Labour Market", in *A Guide to Post-Keynesian Economics*, Alfred Eichner (ed.), M.E. Sharpe: New York: 100-119.

Chick, V. (1983), *Macroeconomics after Keynes*, Cambridge, MA: MIT Press.

Das, Shakuntala (2008), "Report on the National Rural Employment Guarantee Act (MGNREGA): West Bengal", *Mimeo*, obtained through personal correspondence with the author.

Dasgupta, A.K. (1954), "Keynesian Economics and Underdeveloped Countries", *Economic and Political Weekly.*

Dev, M.S. (2002), "Bold Initiatives Needed in Agriculture and Rural Employment", *Economic and Political Weekly,* 37(12): 1088-1091.

Forstater, Mathew (1999), "Functional Finance and Full Employment: Lessons from Lerner for Today", *Journal of Economic Issues*, 33 (2): 475-482.

Fullwiler, Scott (2004), "Macroeconomic Stabilization through an Employer of Last Resort", *Centre for Full Employment and Price Stability,* Working Paper 44, available at www.cfeps.org.

Ghosh, J. (2009), *Equity and Inclusion through Public Expenditure: The Potential of the NREGS,* Pragati.

Ghosh, S., Trishna Satpathy and Aasha Kapur (2008), "National Rural Employment Guarantee Scheme", *Alternative Economic Survey, India 2007-08*, 223.

Keynes, John M., (1936), *The General Theory of Employment, Interest, and Money,* New York: Harcourt, Brace, Jovanovich.

Kregel, J.A. (1987), "The Effective Demand Approach to Employment and Inflation", *Journal of Post-Keynesian Economics*, 10(1): 133-145.

Lerner, Abba (1943), "Functional Finance and the Federal Debt", *Social Research* 10 (1), 38-51.

Lerner, Abba (1944), *The Economics of Control*, New York: Macmillan.

Marcuzzo, M.C. (2006), "Keynes and the Welfare State", *mimeo.*

Minsky, Hyman (1965), "The Role of Employment Policy", in Margaret Gordon (ed.) *Poverty in America*, San Francisco: Chandler Publishing Company.

Minsky, P. (1986), *Can "It" Happen Again?: Essays in Instability and Finance*, Armonk, New York: M.E. Sharpe.

Mitchell, William (2001), "Fiscal Policy and the Job Guarantee", Working Paper No. 01/09. Newcastle, Australia, Centre for Full Employment and Equity.

Rao, V.K.R.V. (1952), "Investment, Income and the Multiplier in an Underdeveloped Economy", *Indian Economic Review.*

Riach, Peter (1995), "Wage-employment Determination in Post-Keynesian World", in Philip Arestis and Mike Marshal (eds.), *The Political Economy of Full Employment*, Aldershot: Edward Elgar, 163-175.

Rima, Ingrid (2003), The Operational Role of Functional Finance for Labour Market Behaviour and Outcomes in Edward Nell and Mathew Forstater (ed.) *Reinventing Functional Finance: Transformational Growth and Full Employment*, Edward Elgar: Northampton, MA, 266-78.

Shah Mihir (2009), "Multiplier Accelerator Synergy in NREGA", *The Hindu.*

Todorova, Zdravka (2007), "Deficits and Institutional Theorizing about Households and the State", *Journal of Economic Issues*, XLI (2): 319-326.

Vickrey, William (1993), "The Other Side of the Coin", *The American Economist*, 37 (2): 5-16.

Wray, Randall (2007), "The Employer of Last Resort Programme: Could it Work for Developing Countries"?, Economic and Labour Market Papers, *International Labour Office*, Geneva.

3

Financial Inclusion through MGNREGA

Access to finance for those belonging to poor and vulnerable groups is a pre-requisite for poverty reduction and social cohesion. This has to become an integral part of our efforts to promote inclusive growth. In fact, providing access to finance is a form of empowerment of the vulnerable groups. The financial inclusion is the process of ensuring delivery of financial services to vulnerable groups which is timely, adequate and at an affordable cost.

The various financial services include credit, savings, insurance and payments and remittance facilities. MGNREGA was a revolutionary step in its promise of inclusive growth and financial inclusion, the right to work and the dignity of labour and a rational, participatory relationship with the state.

With a view to infuse transparency and enhancing the integrity of wage payment under MGNREGA, and also to encourage savings among the rural poor, Schedule II of MGNREGA Act was amended to make wage disbursement to MGNREGA workers through institutional accounts in banks or post offices as a statutory requirement. Wage payments through MGNREGA have initiated the biggest "financial inclusion" drive, with the requirement that all wage payments be made through banks and post offices. Payment of wages to workers employed under MGNREGA can be done with speed, reliability, low transaction costs and leakages, if each worker has a bank account in which wages are transferred periodically. With the implementation of MGNREGA, large flow of funds is occurring from government to the rural households, which has opened up a new chapter in the history of rural development in India.

3.1 Wage Payment through Banks

The wage payments through banks and post offices (POs) had been a step forward in many ways, notably by enabling millions of people to open bank or post office accounts and by making it much hard for corrupt middlemen to embezzle wage funds. It separates the implementing agency from the payment agency. Hence, as against direct payment of cash to the labourers by the panchayat/block authorities (or even contractors), who could keep a share of the money for themselves, in the banking system, the money goes directly into the account of the labourers. This would also discourage corrupt authorities from fudging the muster rolls. Moreover, the payment through banks and post offices would promote the habit of savings among rural unskilled workers.

According to a recent announcement, under the new system of financial inclusion, 10.02 crore accounts of MGNREGA workers have been opened and about 90 percent of wages have been disbursed through these accounts up to March 2014—accounting for 75 percent of the expenditure under the programme. Such huge flow of funds from the government treasury to poor rural households provides an immense opportunity to bring the beneficiaries into the fold of organized banking system.

Although this new system has been hailed as a foolproof, cost-effective solution to reduce leakages and to promote greater transparency, the transition was rushed and several complications with the new system are now becoming apparent.

As per 2013-14 data, there were more than 1,000 banks working in different parts of country, managing 10.02 crore accounts of MGNREGA workers—the largest financial inclusion scheme of the rural poor by which wages are disbursed through this account. These accounts have also encouraged thrift and savings among some of the poorest families. The state-wise and bank-wise details of number of accounts opened for MGNREGA wage payment is shown in

Table 3.1.

Table: 3.1: Number of Accounts in all Banks under MGNREGA (2013-14)

S. No.	States	Banks			
		Commercial	RRBs	Cooperative	Total
1.	Andaman and Nicobar Islands	11399	0	4	11403
2.	Andhra Pradesh	3205858	0	0	3205858
3.	Arunachal Pradesh	25901	10520	20260	56681
4.	Assam	861242	664612	47402	1573256
5.	Bihar	1034897	373177	38598	1446672
6.	Chhattisgarh	1418697	788633	451443	2658773
7.	Goa	15469	0	2820	18289
8.	Gujarat	702158	85972	26522	814652
9.	Haryana	422854	194617	151784	769255
10.	Himachal Pradesh	321473	133798	398635	853906
11.	Jammu and Kashmir	910541	120403	122880	1153824
12.	Jharkhand	464438	74891	102728	642057
13.	Karnataka	2377895	1688401	9295	4075591
14.	Kerala	1578483	351473	215333	2145289
15.	Lakshadweep	1257	0	0	1257
16.	Madhya Pradesh	3850598	1312766	596140	5759504
17.	Maharashtra	1297864	341263	533488	2172615
18.	Manipur	133972	47955	13351	195278
19.	Meghalaya	17651	27071	4787	49509
20.	Mizoram	3105	78269	3745	85119
21.	Nagaland	70	0	4	74
22.	Odisha	2652967	972556	59295	3684818
2.3	Puducherry	64453	11800	1172	77425
24.	Punjab	717704	96343	45466	859513
25.	Rajasthan	884624	692340	3630008	5206972
26.	Sikkim	34712	0	32666	67378
27.	Tamil Nadu	7567495	567996	2354	8137845
28.	Tripura	99634	441696	218853	760183
29.	Uttar Pradesh	5158588	4898361	199307	10256256
30.	Uttarakhand	326770	117740	137508	582018
31.	West Bengal	4815806	1409724	576708	6802238
	Grand Total	**40980804**	**15502377**	**7642556**	**64125737**

Source: www.nrega.nic.in

3.2 Index of Financial Inclusion (IFI) through MGNREGA

For constructing the index of financial inclusion (IFI), several indicators have been used to assess the extent of financial inclusion through the implementation of MGNREGA. The most commonly used indicator is availability of banking services, banking penetration and banking disbursement. A comprehensive measure of financial inclusion should be able to incorporate information on several dimensions of financial inclusion, preferably in one single number. Such a measure can be used to compare the levels of financial inclusion across economies and across states/provinces within countries at a particular time point. This tool can be used to monitor the progress of MGNREGA wage payment as a measure of financial inclusion in the country over a period of time. The various dimensions of IFI are follows.

3.2.1 Availability of Banking Services (Dimension D_1): The services of an inclusive financial system should be easily available to its users. Availability of services can be indicated by the number of bank outlets and/or by the number of ATM per 1,000 people, or the number of bank employees per customer. In the absence of comparable data on the number of ATMs and number of bank staff for a large number of states, we use the number of banks where MGNREGA wage transactions take place to measure the availability dimension. There are about 1,000 banks working across the country where banking services are available to the MGNREGA workers.

3.2.2 Banking Penetration (Dimension D_2): An inclusive financial system should have as many users as possible, that is, an inclusive financial system should penetrate widely amongst its users. The size of the "banked" population, i.e. number of people having a bank account is a measure of the banking penetration of the system. Thus, if every person in an economy has a bank account, then the value of this measure would be 1. Here, we are considering the number of MGNREGA workers who have bank accounts as an indicator of this dimension.

3.2.3 Banking Disbursement (Dimension D_3): The wage payments through banks makes millions of people develop the habit of banking and inclusion in the financial system. We are considering here the amount of MGNREGA wages disbursed through bank accounts. With the number of 10.02 crore accounts for MGNREGA workers, this becomes the largest financial inclusion scheme of the rural poor by which wages are disbursed through this account.

The proposed IFI takes values between 0 and 1, zero indicating lowest financial inclusion (complete financial exclusion) and 1 indicating complete financial inclusion. Such an index, in our view, will be most useful for policy makers and academic researchers. The dimension index for the ith dimension, d_i, is computed by the following formula.

$$D_i = \frac{Ai - mi}{Mi - mi} \quad (1)$$

Where,

A_i = Actual value of dimension i

m_i = Minimum value of dimension i

M_i = Maximum value of dimension i

Thus, considering the above three dimensions—number of banks, number of bank accounts under MGNREGA and amount of wage disbursed through bank—we can represent a state i by a point (d_1, d_2, d_3) in the three dimensional Cartesian space, such that $0 < d_1, d_2, d_3 < 1$, where d_1, d_2 and d_3 denote the dimension indices for country i computed using above formula. In the three dimensional Cartesian space, the point (0,0,0) indicates the worst situation (complete financial exclusion) and the point (1,1,1) indicates the best or ideal situation (complete financial inclusion). The IFI for the state i is measured by the normalized inverse Euclidean distance of the point (d1, d2, d3) from the ideal point (1,1,1). Algebraically,

$$\text{IFI} = 1 - \sqrt{((1 - D1)^2 + (1 - D2)^2 + (1 - D3)^2)/3} \quad (2)$$

While computing an index such as the one proposed here, availability of data is an important challenge. We find that the latest year for which some data are available for a reasonable number of states is the financial year 2013-14. Using data on all three dimensions for 25 states for the year 2013-14, IFI values have been computed. The IFI values computed for various states are presented in Table 3.2.

Table 3.2: Index of Financial Inclusion using Data on 3 Dimensions (2013-14)

S. No.	States	No. of Banks	No. of Workers with Accounts	Wages Disbursed through Bank Accounts (₹ lakh)
1.	Andhra Pradesh	3	11800699	53025.64
2.	Arunachal Pradesh	6	81642	2193.77
3.	Assam	44	2674380	27719.94
4.	Bihar	42	4882384	38627.05
5.	Chhattisgarh	79	6843768	56750.09
6.	Goa	24	18294	204.17
7.	Gujarat	39	2317929	14083.85
8.	Haryana	42	812667	23308.71
9.	Himachal Pradesh	42	890902	34460.9
10.	Jammu & Kashmir	47	1173799	35819.64
11.	Jharkhand	35	3154097	10534.88
12.	Karnataka	51	4687310	137698.77
13.	Kerala	48	2242120	100485.52
14.	Madhya Pradesh	58	7446237	119241.45
15.	Maharashtra	52	4191755	45348.14
16.	Mizoram	5	160394	6151.64
17.	Odisha	46	5266954	73696.38
18.	Punjab	44	957354	16014.55
19.	Rajasthan	48	9461736	115287.58
20.	Sikkim	17	97122	4042.17
21.	Tamil Nadu	41	8138266	0
22.	Tripura	14	818676	62855.2
23.	Uttar Pradesh	63	10754235	203567.85
24.	Uttarakhand	48	773219	15315.82
25.	West Bengal	81	12041310	133432.69

Contd...

States	D_1	D_2	D_3	IFI	Rank
Uttar Pradesh	0.769231	0.892949	1	0.853128	1
West Bengal	1	1	0.655124	0.800886	2
Madhya Pradesh	0.705128	0.61781	0.585342	0.632595	3
Rajasthan	0.576923	0.785447	0.565899	0.628754	4
Karnataka	0.615385	0.38834	0.676102	0.542847	5
Tamil Nadu	0.487179	0.675369	0.420865	0.515656	6
Chhattisgarh	0.974359	0.567701	0.278053	0.513945	7
Odisha	0.551282	0.436551	0.361383	0.444226	8
Kerala	0.576923	0.184964	0.493113	0.394412	9
Maharashtra	0.628205	0.347123	0.221986	0.375557	10
Bihar	0.5	0.404565	0.188937	0.351318	11
Andhra Pradesh	0	0.979987	0.259739	0.281579	12
Assam	0.525641	0.220917	0.135303	0.274354	13
Jammu & Kashmir	0.564103	0.096108	0.175132	0.250014	14
Jharkhand	0.410256	0.260817	0.050799	0.226443	15
H. Pradesh	0.5	0.072578	0.168451	0.225062	16
Gujarat	0.461538	0.191269	0.068251	0.222795	17
Haryana	0.5	0.066071	0.113612	0.202523	18
Uttarakhand	0.576923	0.06279	0.074308	0.201196	19
Punjab	0.525641	0.078105	0.077744	0.198863	20
Tripura	0.141026	0.066571	0.308074	0.165756	21
Goa	0.269231	0	0	0.080938	22
Sikkim	0.179487	0.006556	0.018873	0.064981	23
Mizoram	0.025641	0.011819	0.029245	0.022206	24
Arunachal Pradesh	0.038462	0.005269	0.009783	0.017728	25

Depending on the value of IFI, states are categorized into three categories, viz.

1. 0.5 < IFI < 1 - high financial inclusion.
2. 0.3 < IFI < 0.5 - medium financial inclusion.
3. 0 < IFI < 0.3 - low financial inclusion.

As shown in Table 3.2, the highest number of banks is in West Bengal followed by Chhattisgarh, Uttar Pradesh and Madhya Pradesh. However, if we look at the number of MGNREGA workers who have bank accounts, West Bengal ranks the highest followed by Andhra Pradesh, Uttar Pradesh, Rajasthan, and Tamil Nadu. Looking at another dimension of an inclusive banking system, that is, amount of MGNREGA wages disbursed through bank account, Uttar Pradesh seems to have the highest followed by Karnataka and West Bengal. As evident from this example, any single indicator fails to adequately capture the extent of financial inclusion. Therefore, a comprehensive measure of financial inclusion should be able to incorporate information on several aspects of financial inclusion which can be used to compare the levels of financial inclusion across economies and across states within countries at a particular time point.

Thus, we propose an index of financial inclusion (IFI), which takes into account the above three criteria. The proposed IFI takes values between 0 and 1, 0 indicating lowest financial inclusion and 1 indicating complete financial inclusion.

In the group of 25 states for which a 3-dimensional IFI has been estimated by using data on 3 dimensions of financial inclusion, Uttar Pradesh leads with the highest value of IFI with values of 0.853 (Table 3.2). Only seven states belong to the high IFI group. The other six states are, West Bengal, Madhya Pradesh, Rajasthan, Karnataka, Tamil Nadu and Chhattisgarh form the group of highest IFI states with IFI values between 0.5 and 1. Another four states, viz. Odisha, Kerala, Maharashtra and Bihar form the group of Medium IFI states with IFI values between 0.3 and 0.5. All other states have a low IFI values, lying between 0.01 and 0.3. It is interesting to note that most of the states having highest participation and awareness about the scheme have high and medium IFI values.

Adequate, appropriate and comparable data for a large number of years and for a large number of states is the essence of a robust IFI. Owing to lack of appropriate data, we are unable to incorporate many aspects of an inclusive financial system in our present index, such as affordability, timeliness and quality of the financial services.

3.3 Benefits and Problems of Bank Payments

- Reduced cost of payment delivery for the government if new accounts are opened for recipients or alternative payment channels are used.
- Recipients need not go out of their way to receive payments.
- Payments delivered more quickly.
- Reduction in number of fictitious or duplicate beneficiaries.
- Reduction in cases of fraud where funds are siphoned off without recipients' awareness as it separates the implementing agency from the payment agency.
- Avoidance of middlemen or agents for transaction.
- Relationship with financial system.
- Social recognition.
- Access to financial products for economic growth and well-being.

The switch to bank payments has undoubtedly provided substantial protection against embezzlement and is a critical step towards ensuring greater accountability in the disbursement of wages under MGNREGA. However, these payments are getting delayed for various reasons. One is that either the banks are unwilling to cope with the load or they are unable to cope with the load. Just look at the plight of a bank—a rural branch where they would get, may be 70 or 80 customers in a day, and suddenly with transfer of MGNREGA wages, an upwards of 500 beneficiaries seeking their payments turning up on the same day week after week. Such situations lead to work overload in banks and post offices, exacerbating the delays and inconvenience. Lot of pressure on bank manpower on account of MGNREGA accounts and other government benefit accounts has resulted in high costs and low return on such accounts. Regular banking business/regular customer service has been affected on account of heavy rush on payment days. Thus, it is an important cause for severe delays in the disbursement of wages, i.e. the institutional incapacity of rural banks to handle the large volume of accounts. The shortage of staff and technology is most acute in post offices where accounts are managed manually through log journals.

The poor maintenance of bank/post office passbooks, makes it difficult for workers to keep track of their wages, and for social auditors to verify the payment details. Many states still lack well-designed "payment orders" (sometimes payment orders are designed by hand on the spot). It is a well-established argument that the coverage of banks and post offices in rural India is patchy and as a consequence, workers especially in remote parts of the country find it difficult to travel long distances to collect their wages thereby causing delays in payments. But, interestingly findings from a survey in U.P. and Jharkhand indicate that approximately 90 percent of workers who lived more than 5 km. from a bank/post office expressed a preference for bank payments over cash despite the distance, indicating that the problems lie elsewhere which has led to major inconvenience including extra spending of time and money in making frequent journeys to the bank/post office for MGNREGA workers in cases where there is no bank or post office within a reasonable distance. The system of "wage slips", recommended in the MGNREGA Operational Guidelines, is non-functional (if it has been introduced at all) in many states.

It has generally been found that extremely few MGNREGA workers surveyed, had pre-existing bank accounts. In cases where bank accounts were opened for the workers in order to deliver MGNREGA wages, the workers seldom used the accounts for anything other than receiving their wages. Payments of MGNREGA workers continue to be made through non-bank channels such as post offices or Gram Panchayats in many parts of the country despite central government requirements that wages should be paid through bank accounts. It is mainly because of lack of awareness about financial facilities (financial illiteracy). For a sustainable financial inclusion, financial literacy becomes a very critical component. There is a need to simultaneously focus on the financial literacy part besides delivery/access.

The other problem, of course, is that MGNREGA as a scheme does not provide additional money to handle the transaction fee. Why would the banks want to undertake this responsibility given the costs involved? Banks are commercial entities—who have to answer to shareholders—a bank's chairman's career graph depends on what the bank's bottom line looks like. They have to make some money in the process of handling MGNREGA payments, which entail small amounts that just come in and go out of the bank. Somebody working under MGNREGA is unlikely to have a substantial savings account. Only in states like Andhra Pradesh, state government has been proactive and has provided for 2 percent of the money to be given to the banks for handling MGNREGA payments.

In other states, this is not the case. Hence, the viability is a big issue and a recurrent one in various discussions and meetings encountered. Thus, the issue of delays in wage payments is one of the most serious problems with the system of bank payments. Reports from several states including Jharkhand, West Bengal, Chhattisgarh, Rajasthan, Madhya Pradesh, Uttar Pradesh and West Bengal indicate the problem of delayed payments and dwindling interest in employment under the MGNREGA as a rampant problem. Despite the spread of rural bank branches, large number of rural households still do not have any access to banking services.

More than 50 percent of the adult population in rural areas still do not have bank accounts.

3.4 Branchless Banking and Business Correspondent Model

The increase in the number of branches has not answered the needs of the poor; and reaching the unbanked population to enable inclusive growth is a serious problem today. Branchless banking could be a big step towards providing easy financial access to the poor people and achieving financial inclusion. In order to promote financial inclusion amongst the unbanked, the Reserve Bank of India (RBI) has developed a set of guidelines to formalize branchless banking, which they call the business correspondent (BC) model. Under this framework, banks can partner with third party agents to provide financial services such as credit and savings on their behalf. It is a concept of providing banking services outside the conventional bank branches by either using information or communication technology services or the services of non-governmental organisations, self-help groups, micro finance institutions and other civil society organisations as intermediaries to handle account opening, transaction management, and other financial services through the use of business facilitator and correspondent models. The business correspondent scheme would generate employment opportunities for the local educated youth who would work as business correspondents. They will be available to help the workers at the gram panchayat level on weekdays and would have flexible working hours.

The 'business correspondent model' which is currently being rolled out by the government is an attempt to address this problem of delayed payments and ensure that the rural poor have timely access to financial services under MGNREGA. How this works is that the business correspondent (BC) would, on behalf of the banks, for a commission, deliver financial services to 'clients' though appropriate technology like handheld computer devices.

However, given that the problem of delays is more complex than a simple issue of institutional access, the solutions might lie beyond the scope of this administrative 'innovation'. The features of the business correspondent model are:

- Banks permitted to outsource transaction processing to certain types of organisations (non-profit organisations and co-operatives allowed; NBFCs not allowed).
- All transaction information required to be updated in bank's CBS by the end of day.
- Agents must be located within 15 kilometres of a partner bank branch.

The BC model is in its infancy. Different experiments are being tried out to enhance the understanding and the skill sets of the sector to make the model a viable and a feasible instrument of increasing financial services outreach. In the initial stages, the focus seems to be on inclusion. However, allowing BCs to handle cash is the biggest challenge. Ninety-nine percent of the financial transactions are in cash, warranting high-cost cash-handling operations and added operational risks. Moreover, clients tend to perceive that the BCs are the owners of the transactions and are not facilitating them on banks' behalf. Irregularities have been observed in accounting of clients' withdrawals and deposits by BCs and as a result there have been delays in accounting of the banking transactions. The BCs and bank staff operate individually without any supervision, hence, the risk of fraud and misappropriation is higher.

The banking correspondent model is meant to provide affordable banking facility (deposits, advances and remittances) to the unbanked population. Currently, of around 6 lakh villages in India, only 30,000 villages have a bank branch. Since, sometimes opening of a bank branch is not viable, after a consultative process, RBI introduced the BC model for providing ICT-based financial inclusion. With the available smart card technology/IT infrastructure, it was felt that formal banking facility can be provided to the unbanked villages through information and communication technology driven BC model. BCs could be any entities such as civil society organisations or not-for-profit companies (except an NBFC) who can work on behalf of the bank including transacting cash with the account holders.

3.5 Smartcard Payment Scheme of FINO

Technology companies including, Financial Information Networks and Operations (FINO) and A Little World, now using the business correspondent model to deliver MGNREGA wages and pensions in several districts of Andhra Pradesh, found that the introduction of the new payment system has achieved significant results including reduced delivery time for beneficiaries, beneficiaries spending less waiting time in line for payments to be processed, increased empowerment of female beneficiaries as payments (no longer disbursed to husbands or brothers) and reduced leakage due to fictitious or duplicate pensioners. FINO, in collaboration with the state government of Andhra Pradesh and several partner banks, has delivered payments from MGNREGA to beneficiaries using a platform based on smartcards and mobile smartcard readers. The smartcard payment system has resulted in greater convenience and empowerment for beneficiaries and reduced fraud at the back end. With the smartcard payment scheme, beneficiaries spend fewer days waiting for payments to become available and less time waiting in line at transaction points for their payments to be processed.

From the beneficiary's perspective, the process of receiving MGNREGA wages or social security pensions via a smartcard is simple and, superficially, similar to receiving payments via a post office savings account. Each Thursday or Friday, the beneficiary visits the local Gram Panchayat office with his or her smartcard where a trained agent, or "customer service provider" (CSP), equipped with a FINO-designed point of transaction (POT) device awaits the beneficiary.

The CSP swipes the beneficiary's smartcard, takes the

beneficiary's fingerprints using a built-in fingerprint reader to confirm his or her identity, and then gives the beneficiary the amount listed on the POT screen. After the transaction is complete, the POT device automatically prints two receipts for the transaction, one of which is signed by the CSP and given to the beneficiary and the other is stored by the CSP. The entire transaction takes around one minute to perform.

3.6 ZMF by ALW

FINO's partner organisation A Little World (ALW) developed a technology solution to deliver MGNREGA wages. Zero Microfinance and Savings Support Foundation (ZMF) has tied up with seven banks for delivering payments via smartcards in Andhra Pradesh. ZMF staffs carry a single mobile phone along with a fingerprint reader capable of communicating with the phone via bluetooth. ZMF staff records most client details through the use of paper-based forms, with only the beneficiary's fingerprints, photo, and voice recording of the person's name being captured digitally. According to ZMF, this low footprint approach allows them to save costs as laptops, digital cameras, and portable generators are no longer required for conducting enrolment.

The technology used by ZMF staff for processing payments is similar to that used by FINO but differs in two key ways. First, rather than a single point of sale device, ZMF agents utilize three separate components when processing the payments: a mobile phone, a fingerprint reader, and a receipt printer. In practice, these three components communicate automatically with one other so that for all practical purposes, operating the components is equivalent to operating a single POT device. According to ZMF, a primary benefit of this technology setup is that the process of uploading and downloading payment and transaction information is greatly simplified as data can be sent automatically by the mobile phone. ZMF management claim that weekly uploads and downloads take no more than two minutes and can even be processed in the background while the agent conducts other tasks on the phone. One potential drawback of this method of data transmission however is that the technology required for transmitting data via the mobile networks (GPRS) has not been installed in all mobile base stations in India. According to ALW and ZMF management, this has not been a problem till date as all agents have been able to access a GPRS signal either within their village or by travelling a short distance.

Second, the smartcards disbursed by ZMF are contact less NFC (near field communication) cards rather than contact cards like those disbursed by FINO. NFC smartcards are slightly more expensive than contact smartcards but provide the advantage that they must only be waved in front of the mobile phone (or other reader) rather than inserted and allow for significantly faster data transmission between the card and reader (less than a second for NFC vs. around 5 seconds for contact smartcards). In terms of the smartcard reader, there is little difference in cost between a device capable of reading NFC cards and the one capable of reading contact cards.

3.7 Wage Payment through Cheque under MGNREGA

To increase transparency and accountability in the MGNREGA process, a new system of payment through cheques has been put in place. Under the scheme, the administration has distributed *shramik* coupons, designed to look like a commercial bank's cheque book. Each cheque, with a counterfoil, has a value of MGNREGA wage rate. The use of the cheque books can be viewed under two situations: cash payments and payment through banks.

In the first case, the villages where the MGNREGA beneficiary does not have a bank account or for some reason the payment is not done through the bank, the MGNREGA cheque book is being used in the following manner. At the time of payment, a worker submits to the *gram rozgar sevak*, the number of coupons equal to the number of days he has worked. In second case, though opening of bank accounts is an ideal method for the payment of wages, it does not weed away some of the practical problems in MGNREGA. For instance, there might be a case where the labourer is not paid for the total number of days he worked or that he is not paid in time. At the end of each day, a worker asks the *gram rozgar sevak* to put the MGNREGA seal on the counter foil. The worker keeps the counter foil and gives the cheque to the *sevak.*

3.8 Electronic Benefit Transfer (EBT) through Banks

To encourage banks to adopt information and communication technology (ICT) solutions for enhancing their outreach, the RBI formulated a scheme to quicken the pace of adoption of the smart card-based electronic benefit transfer (EBT) mechanism by banks and rolled out the EBT system in the states that are ready to adopt the scheme. As per the scheme, the RBI would reimburse the banks a part of the cost of opening accounts with bio-metric access/smart cards at the rate of ₹ 50 per account through which payment of social security benefits, MGNREGA payments and payments under other government benefit programmes would be routed to persons belonging to below poverty line (BPL) families. The scheme was implemented in Andhra Pradesh. Seven banks were paid ₹ 1.8 crore for smart cards issued by banks in Andhra Pradesh during July-December 2008. The process is at different stages of implementation in other states such as Karnataka and Uttarakhand and the scheme of partial reimbursement by the Reserve Bank was extended by one year up to June 30, 2010.

Banks are advised to work in co-ordination with the respective government departments at the Central and State levels to ensure that all State benefits are delivered to individuals only through bank accounts within a specific timeframe.

Similar caution is required with related innovations such as the use of smart cards, biometric identification, etc., to facilitate wage payments. Some of these innovations are likely to be very valuable in due course, but they require careful experimentation, and one must always guard against undue reliance on them as well as against hasty transitions to new arrangements that may not be adequately tested. The hasty "switch" to bank (and post office) payments in mid-2008, which caused havoc for several months, was a sobering experience in this regard. Its lessons should not be forgotten.

3.9 Biometric ATM for MGNREGA Workers

Basic bank accounts are something that most of the rural people take for granted. Majority of the rural households do not have bank account mainly because of less family earnings. This results in an economic disadvantage. To reach the rural masses and to boost micro financing initiatives, biometric ATMs with secured finger print readers are hitting the rural villages. This biometric ATM is equipped with biometric sensor which has finger print authentications as a standard feature and it is possible for the illiterate or semi-literate folks to use just thumb impression on a touch screen which will allow the beneficiaries to withdraw their week's wages. The ATM accepts finger prints as the means of authentication instead of PIN numbers only as used by other ATMs. This ensures that the biometric ATM is very easy to use. It rules out the possibility of leakages in the payment as the entire wages are disbursed through the bank.

This project will demonstrate the significant reduction of cash delivery time, prevention of leakages and pilferages and promotion of transparency in the system. In case of payment through the bank branches, the workers have to wait in long queues. They are also not properly attended by the bank staff. Besides, most of the bank branches are running short of staff. There these workers are perceived by the banking system as an additional burden on them and the workers are ill-treated in many cases. The above system will encourage more savings as the amount goes directly to the bank and the workers can withdraw a minimum amount or whatever they require rather than the entire amount. The pilot project has been initiated in states like Andhra Pradesh, Kerala, Uttar Pradesh, Bihar and Odisha.

Thus, MGNREGA provides a greater opportunity to the government for financial inclusion and inclusive growth. The wage payments through banks and post office had led to greater transparency and reliability for payments and increase in banking habits among rural people of India. However, even the increase in branches is not a solution to enhanced financial inclusion—as a large number of rural poor are still unable to get financial facilities—appropriate innovation and introduction of modern technology will work as a facilitator and business correspondent. Even today, financial inclusion of mass rural people for inclusive growth is a greater challenge for policy makers, planners and economic elites.

References

Binit, Rath, Minakshi Ramji and Alexandra Kobishyn (2009), "Business Correspondent Model: A Preliminary Exploration", Centre for Micro Finance at *IFMR*.

Discussion Paper (2010), "Rights-based Legal Guarantee as Development Policy: The Mahatma Gandhi National Rural Employment Guarantee Act", *UNDP*.

Ghate, Pabhu (2008), "Branchless Banking in India", *The Economic Times*. Available at, http://economictimes.indiatimes.com/Opinion/Branchless_banking_in_India/rssarticleshow/3386737.cms.

Johnson, Doug (2008), "Case Study on the Use of Smartcards to Deliver Government Benefits in Andhra Pradesh, India", Centre for Micro Finance, *IFMR*.

Kochhar, Sameer (2010), "Speeding Financial Inclusion", *SKOCH Development Foundation*.

Prasad, Rajkumar (2009), "NERGA and ICT for Poverty Reduction and Rural People Employment in India".

Rajanish, Dass, (2011), "Workshop on Role of ICT in Financial Inclusion", *IIM* Ahmedabad.

Reddy, Narasimha D. and Upendranath, C. (2010), "National Rural Employment Guarantee: Issues, Concerns and Prospects", Study Supported by Oxfam India in collaboration with Institute for Human Development, New Delhi.

Sarma Mandira (2008), "Index of Financial Inclusion", Working Paper No. 215, *Indian Council for Research on International Economic Relations.*

4

Wages under MGNREGA

The Mahatma Gandhi National Rural Employment Guarantee Act (MGNREGA) is the first ever law internationally, that guarantees wage employment on an unprecedented scale. MGNREGA aims at enhancing livelihood security of households in rural areas of the country by providing at least one hundred days of guaranteed wage employment in a financial year to every household whose adult members volunteer to do unskilled manual work. Unique features of the Act include: time bound employment guarantee and wage payment within 15 days; incentive-disincentive structure to the state government for providing employment as 90 percent of the cost for employment provided is borne by the Centre or payment of unemployment allowance at their own cost and emphasis on labour intensive works prohibiting the use of contractors, and machinery. The Act also mandates 33 percent participation for women.

4.1 Initial Phase

In the initial phase (2006 and 2007) of the implementation of MGNREGA, it was seen that workers were not attracted towards this scheme as the actual wage payment was relatively below the prescribed minimum wages. The national average number of days of employment given to eligible households hovered around 45 days as against the guaranteed 100 days in these years. This was because in most of the states the schedule of rates was quite old and had been calculated when contractors and machines were utilised. Under MGNREGA, contractors and machines are banned and all jobs have to be accomplished through manual labour.

The Act has augmented household income and the average

wage rate has increased from ₹ 65 in financial year 2006-07 to ₹ 136 in 2014-15. Post-MGNREGA, there has been a revision of minimum wage for agricultural labourers across the country. In order to increase transparency and bring the rural poor under the organized banking sector and credit system, agencies for wage payment are being separated from implementing agencies through accounts-based wage payment. Initial experiments in the use of smart cards and biometric signatures for wage payment to MGNREGA workers in remote villages are being supported.

Research institutions and non-governmental organizations (NGOs) collected evidence of lower-than-minimum wages under MGNREGA and advocated for a revision of the schedule of rates and daily wages by conducting a fresh time and motion study. They advocated this need through the media, multi-stakeholder dialogue, petitions and court cases to the state governments. All this led to the notification of a new schedule of rates based on the time and motion study resulting in an increase in wages in recent years.

4.2 Provisions Related to Wages under MGNREGA

Section 3.2 of the Act says that every person who has done the work given to him/her under the Scheme shall be entitled to receive wages at the wage rate for each day of work. Notwithstanding provisions contained in the Minimum Wages Act, 1948, the Central Government may, by notification, specify the wage rate for the purposes of this Act provided that the wage rate specified from time to time under any such notification shall not be at a rate less than ₹ 60 per day (Section 6.1). Until such time as a wage rate is fixed by the Central Government in respect of any area in a state, the minimum wage fixed by the state government under Section 3 of the Minimum Wages Act, 1948, for agricultural labourers shall be considered as the wage rate applicable to that area. This minimum wage for agricultural labourers varies from state to state. The Government of India has stated its commitment to provide a wage rate of ₹ 100.

Under no circumstances the labourers shall be paid less than the wage rate (Section 6 of Schedule I). When wages are directly linked with the quantity of work, the wages shall be paid according to the schedule of rates fixed by the state government for different types of work every year, in consultation with the State Employment Guarantee Council. Another notification of the Union Ministry of Rural Development issued on January 14, 2008 has made significant amendments in Schedule I of the MGNREGA.

The original paragraph 8 of this Schedule, "the schedule of rates of wages for unskilled labourers shall be so fixed that a person working for seven hours would normally earn a wage equal to the wage rate" has now been replaced by, "8(1): The schedule of rates of wages for various unskilled labourers shall be so fixed that an adult person working for nine hours would normally earn a wage equal to the wage rate; 8(2): The working days of an adult worker shall be so arranged that inclusive of intervals or rest, if any, it shall not spread over more than twelve hours on any day".

The notification also says that after paragraph 8, the following paragraph shall be inserted: "8(A): The average out-turns of work put out by men and women workers working in a group will be the basis for fixing a task-based schedule of rates so that there is no gender-based discrimination in the Schedule of Rates". Subsequently, through its Circular No. J-11011/2/2007, NREGA, the Ministry of Rural Development, Government of India, clarified, "doubt has been raised in certain quarters about the period of interval of rest in the above-referred notification. It is clarified that nine hours of work is inclusive of one hour of interval of rest". Hence, as of now, for calculating a day's work, state authorities are supposed to consider eight hours of work".

Section 30 of Schedule II says that in case the payment of wages is not made within the period specified under the Scheme, the labourers shall be entitled to receive payment of compensation as per the provisions of the Payment of Wages Act, 1936 (4 of 1936). The wages under a scheme may be paid either wholly in cash or in cash and kind provided that at least one fourth of the wages shall be paid in cash only (Section 31 of Schedule II).

The state government may prescribe that a portion of the wages in cash may be paid to the labourers on a daily basis during the period of employment (Section 32 of Schedule II). However, labourers are not being paid in kind in any state.

4.3 MGNREGA and Rural Poverty

With the increase in employment opportunities and wage rates under MGNREGA, there has been a significant dent in poverty in rural areas. At the national level, average wage paid under MGNREGA has increased from ₹ 65 (2006-07) to ₹ 136 in 2014-15. This has led to the strengthening of the livelihood resource base of the rural poor in India.

According to studies of 10 districts of six states by G.B. Pant Social Scienҫe Institute under the coordination of Jean Dreze (2009), the implementation of the Act in the first three years has been able to reach the socially and economically deprived sections as reflected in their participation.

The wage rates under MGNREGA have been further increased by the Ministry of Rural Development with effect from January 1, 2011. This has resulted in 17-35 percent enhancement of wages under this premier flagship program.

The decision to hike wages under MGNREGA comes in the wake of recommendations of National Advisory Council and consultations with the different Ministries. The move is likely to benefit more than 5 crore beneficiaries under MGNREGA across the country. The wage rates have been enhanced on the basis of consumer price index for the agricultural labour calculated on the basis of ₹ 100 or the actual wage rate, whichever is higher as on April 1, 2009. Economists expressed the hope that the decision will go a long way towards meeting of the requirements of the poor in the rural areas across the country.

This upward pressure on rural wages has given rise to two distinct trends. One, workers are finding it better to stay back instead of migrating because of better income at home. In most of the states, the incidence of out-migration was extremely high prior to implementation of MGNREGA. At least one member from each household migrated to different places like Punjab and Haryana for manual work. With the commencement of MGNREGA works, which has ensured employment in their native place, the incidence of out-migration has come down. The income earned through MGNREGA works and the savings which they accumulated by working as migrant labourers in far away places was invested for increasing the paddy yield. Further, the impetus for improving the crop yield came from the fact that they now have to depend on crop cultivation more than when they were migrating out.

Second, given lesser migration there is a difficulty being faced by farmers to get agricultural labourers. A report carried by the Indian Express (2008) succinctly captures this dynamics. Migrant labours from Uttar Pradesh and Bihar have been playing a crucial role in Punjab's agrarian success story. The report points out that in 2006, around 4.21 lakh migrant workers came from these two states alone. The report quotes figures from a study done by Punjab Agricultural University, Ludhiana, which calculated that in 2008 the figures could have reduced to 2.5 lakh. With lesser hands, the prosperous farmers in Punjab have been facing problem with the harvest. The Punjab farmers were paying around ₹ 70-80 while the promised MGNREGA wage would be ₹ 100 a day which was cited by the farmers as the reason for lesser labour availability.

The participation in this programme is expected to contribute to higher consumption and asset accumulation of direct beneficiaries through three channels. First, it directly transfers financial resources to the participating households and increases household income, which would consequently increase total consumption and nutritional intake. Second, increased income encourages the poor households to save and invest, which could eventually help the poor to be involved in diverse productive activities. Third, most of the time, work takes the form of irrigation and land development and the work sites are often in the participants' own fields. That is, participants may be paid for increasing the productivity of their own land. Increased productivity may lead to higher income and consumption.

The additional income has transformed the composition of the food consumption pattern. Very poor families are also able to supplement nutritional items like vegetables and pulses and are having a more balanced diet. The evidences are illustrative and over a period of time, if there is a reduction in the malnourishment of children in MGNREGA Panchayats, the impact of additional income will be sufficiently substantiated. There is a clear tendency of using the additional wage income for the education of children. It builds a case of inherent demand for children's better education.

Most of the MGNREGA benefited families utilized their income for accessing children's education or supplementing with additional facilities to improve the quality of education. This long-term investment of MGNREGA wage income will build the capacity of the families for their upward mobility.

4.4 Impact of MGNREGA Wage on Market Wage Rate

Many of the working poor in India are self-employed, a substantial fraction of poor workers are also casual wage earners. There is thus an urgent need to improve the effectiveness of minimum wages in India. It is observed that "simply legislating a minimum wage will not make it happen" (Murgai and Ravallion, 2005). Ensuring a high rate of compliance normally requires a coherent enforcement strategy based on provision of information, effective labour inspections and sanctions in case of violations. Lack of clear information available to employers and workers about the level of minimum wages, and about possible sanctions in case of violation, also reduces the likelihood of compliance. The greater involvement of worker's organizations and NGOs to ensure that the implementation machinery is effective (Labour Bureau, 2005).

But perhaps the most effective enforcement mechanism in a developing country is coherence with the pay provided through employment guarantee schemes like MGNREGA, especially in Indian context. Murgai and Ravallion (2005) suggest that minimum wage legislation in poor countries can only be made really effective if the government acts as the "employer of last resort" and commits to employ the entire excess supply of unskilled workers at the stipulated minimum wage rate. Indeed, from the perspective of workers, the supply of labour at a wage below the minimum depends on whether a better alternative is available or not. If no minimum wage jobs are available, labour will continue to be supplied at sub-minimum wages. In this section, we try to assess to what extent programmes such as those under MGNREGA can play a key role in fostering compliance with a mandatory minimum wage. The key questions are whether MGNREGA can increase employment, raise wages, and reduce poverty in the rural areas.

The programme provides legal entitlement not only to work on demand but also to be paid minimum wages. Wages under MGNREGA were initially linked to statutory state-level minimum wages for agricultural labourers, and later to the national minimum wage floor. The Act also stipulates that both men and women be paid similar wages, which is a significant policy change from earlier employment guarantee schemes. For many poor rural communities, MGNREGA seems to be the lifeline in the absence of any other employment opportunities. There is some evidence that MGNREGA participants are able to reinvest some of the earnings into farms, increase agricultural productivity and reduce their underemployment, especially among poor households (Saraswat, 2011).

The additional employment created under this programme has reduced underemployment and increased total incomes of the households in rural areas, which is a remarkable feature of the programme. As the scheme provides an alternative source of employment, it might also lead to a reduction in the pool of workers migrating to urban areas for work thereby leading to a rise in wages in urban areas.

Initially, some of the states were evidently paying less than the statutory minimum wage, in violation of the Act (Drèze and Oldiges, 2007). One of these was Rajasthan, which was initially commended for the implementation of MGNREGA, especially as it propagated the right to work and information—although demand for employment was very high, because other works were also providing fewer wages to unskilled manual labourers. However, NGOs raised the issue of low wages and organized protests against this blatant violation of law. Public pressure and regular monitoring of the civil society efforts ensured that the payment process was streamlined. As a result, in Rajasthan, it increased the wage negotiation capacity of the workers and also seems to have increased the bargaining power of the working class in the private sector (Menon, 2008).

What has been the impact of MGNREGA on the wages in rural areas? The average wage paid to workers under MGNREGA has been systematically raised over the years, from ₹ 65 in 2005-06 to ₹ 93 in 2009-10 and to ₹ 136 in 2014-15, adjusting for the cost of living. There is enough evidence to suggest that in many rural areas where MGNREGA has been operational, it has helped to raise the agricultural wage rates (Mehrotra, 2008; Drèze and Khera, 2009; Banerjee, 2011). In Tamil Nadu, MGNREGA wages were higher than the market wage rate and in many of the villages it was observed that workers "demanded to be paid at par with MGNREGA wages to be enticed back into agriculture", which led to a doubling of wages (Jeyarajan, 2011, p. 68).

In many of the villages, there was a cascading effect of MGNREGA in terms of increased agriculture wages, which resulted in a doubling of wage income for women in agriculture, in addition to the wage income from MGNREGA (Jeyarajan, 2011; Dasgupta and Sudarshan, 2011). Actually, this brings out the issue of empowerment too as MGNREGA has allowed workers to fight for their rights. The improvement in wages has also led to an increase in consumption of both food and non-food consumables in some states like Andhra Pradesh (Ravi and Engler, 2009; Liu and Deininger, 2010).

MGNREGA's intervention in the rural labour market has also created labour shortages and raised wages paid by farmers to agricultural labourers (Roy, 2010). In Kerala, MGNREGA work exacerbated agriculture labour shortages, and this had an added effect on pushing up wages in the agricultural sector, moving slowly towards the MGNREGA wage rate (Nair, Sreedharan and Anoopkumar, 2009). In Kerala, the wage rate for women in agricultural work increased from ₹ 80 to ₹ 110. The scheme was successful enough in raising the level of employment and income of the rural households, thereby enhancing their purchasing power. The MGNREGA income has been a substantial supplement to other sources of irregular earnings. Sudarshan, Bhattacharya and Fernandez (2010) also found that MGNREGA has led to an upward movement of female unskilled wages. The shortage of female workers for agricultural work has also led to an increase in wages in the rubber and coconut plantations.

In addition, with payment of better wages under the programme, the bargaining power of the poor or the weakest has gone up. However, some have argued that the rise in wages is not just due to "collective bargaining in certain pockets of the country" but also to the fact that the Central Government pays the wage bill and therefore "state governments have an incentive to raise the minimum wages" (Banerjee, 2011, p. 18). Roy and Dey (2009) argue that the programme actually shows how "the Right to Information (RTI) Act can be woven into the fabric of the delivery system and the whole legal and governance and legal paradigm".

There is no doubt that the impacts and achievements of

MGNREGA have varied across different states, largely depending on the commitment of the local leadership at the village council level, the level of institutional preparedness and governance capacities (Reddy et al., 2010). Nonetheless, it seems probable that MGNREGA—despite having some teething problems—has been able to provide wages at the minimum wage level or at least above the prevailing market wage rate. This has benefited a large proportion of casual workers in the rural areas. Here the role of civil society—activists, academics, media, and policy-makers—has been essential in ensuring effective implementation of the programme, and social justice for the workers through the governance system. In a number of states, the higher MGNREGA wages have also clearly led to higher market wages—especially for agricultural workers—through two different but related mechanisms.

First, MGNREGA has indirectly empowered workers to fight for their rights and provided a space for collective bargaining, especially among the unorganized workers. Banerjee argues that MGNREGA has managed to improve agricultural wages by "providing labour a basis to ask for higher wages" (Banerjee, 2011, p. 18). Second, by attracting a number of low-paid workers into the programme, MGNREGA has led to a shortage of labour for regular agricultural work in some places. This has allowed workers to demand better wages for agricultural work, which clearly resulted in improving their incomes. However, the road towards full compliance with the minimum wage is still a long one and changes will take time. While there are deficiencies in some MGNREGA entitlements and a number of institutional improvements need to be made, the programme is clearly a step in the right direction. This is crucial not only for ensuring better wages but also to tackle poverty.

References

Banerjee, K. (2011), "The Employment Guarantee Scheme in India", in *Amandial*, No. 21 (October).

Bhatia, B. and Dreze, J. (2006), "Employment Guarantee in Jharkhand: Ground Realities", *Economic and Political Weekly*, July 22.

Dasgupta, S. Sudarshan, R. (2011), "Issues in Labour Market Inequality and Women's Participation in India's National Rural Employment Guarantee Programme", *Working Paper No. 98*, Policy Integration Department (Geneva, ILO).

Dey, S. and Bedi, A.S. (2010), "The National Rural Employment Guarantee Scheme in Birbhum", *Economic and Political Weekly*, 45(41), pp. 19-25.

Dreze, J. and Reetika Khera (2009), "The Battle for Employment Guarantee", *Frontline*, National News Magazine, Vol. 26, No. 1.

Dreze, Jean (2009), "Making NREGA Work", *G.B. Pant Social Science Institute*, Allahabad University.

Jandu, N. (2010), "Employment Guarantee and Women's Employment in Rural India", *Working Paper*, Ministry of Rural Development, Government of India.

Jeyarajan, J. (2011), "Women and Pro-Poor Policies in Rural Tamil Nadu: An Examination of Practices and Responses", *Economic and Political Weekly,* 46(43), pp. 64-74.

Johnson, D. (2009), "Does NREGS Help Rural Poor to Cope with Bad Weather?" CMF *Working Paper No. 32*, Chennai, Centre for Microfinance, Institute of Financial Management and Research.

Kannan, K.P. (2005), "Linking Employment Guarantee to Human Development", *Economic and Political Weekly*, October 15.

Khera, Reetika (2008), "Empowerment Guarantee Act", *Economic and Political Weekly,* 43(35), pp. 8-10.

Liu, Y. and Deininger, K. (2011), "Poverty Impacts of India's National Rural Guarantee Scheme: Evidence from Andhra Pradesh", Paper presented at *Agriculture and Applied Economics Association,* Annual Meeting.

Mehrotra, S. (2008), "NREGA Two Years On: Where do We Go from Here"?, Economic *and Political Weekly*, 43(31), pp. 27-35.

Ministry of Rural Development (2008), *The National Rural Employment Guarantee Act 2005: Operation Guidelines 2008*, 3rd edition.

Murgai, R. and Ravallion, M. (2005), "Employment Guarantee in Rural India: What would it Cost and How Much would it Reduce Poverty"?, *Economic and Political Weekly*, 40(31), pp. 3450-3455.

Nair, K.N.; Sreedharan, T.P.; and Anoopkumar, M. (2009), "A Study of National Rural Employment Guarantee Programme in Three

Grama Panchayats of Kasargod District", *Working Paper No. 413*, *Centre for Development Studies*, Trivandrum.

NSSO (2006), "Employment-Unemployment Situation in India 2004-05", *Round 61st, National Sample Survey Organization*, Ministry of Statistics and Programme Implementation, Government of India.

Reddy, D.N.; Tankha, R.; Upendranath, C. and Sharma, A.N. (2010), "National Rural Employment Guarantee as Social Protection", in *IDS Bulletin*, 41(4), pp. 63-76.

Roy, A. (2010), "NREGS Pushes up Minimum Wages in Rajasthan", in *The Hindustan Times*, Jodhpur, 11th April.

Sengupta, A.K. (2009), "The Challenge of Employment in India: An Informal Economy Perspective", National Commission for Enterprises, Government of India, Academic Foundation, New Delhi.

Shah, D. and Mohanty, S. (2010), "Implementation of NREGS during Eleventh Plan in Maharashtra: Experiences, Challenges and Way Forward", *Indian Journal of Agricultural Economics*, 65(3), pp. 540-551.

5

MGNREGA as a Tool for Ecological Regeneration

5.1 Ecological Crisis

The global economic and ecological crises can be seen as an opportunity to fundamentally question our paths of 'development', and move towards ideologies, policies, and practices of ecological sustainability and social equity. India in its current globalizing form, presents a vivid picture of unsustainability. Just as there is an increasing concern that the current path of globalization is yielding too few decent jobs, so is there concern that we cannot continue with growth at the expense of environmental quality. We are therefore in a period of transition searching for the policies and the leadership that can take us into a sustainable development path where social and environmental dimensions of globalization are an integral part of economic policy-making. Transitions in employment structures and in workplaces are central to this process. The economists consider degree of livelihood support of rural people and poor farmers and the suggested indicators include increased opportunity for wage employment, expenditure on food intake, wages higher than the market rates, access to gains of common land for poorest households and enhancement in food grain security.

Environmental degradation, including the pollution of water, land and air, the irreversible loss of biodiversity, the deterioration and exhaustion of natural resources like water, fertile agricultural land, and fish, is one of the most serious threats facing economic and broader sustainable development. The environmental and health costs already often outweigh the gains from the economic activity causing the damage. Such degradation will, in the future, be exacerbated by the impacts of climate change, which are already felt in many developing countries. Scientific scenarios for avoiding dangerous and possibly unmanageable climate change require global emissions of greenhouse gases to peak over the next 10-15 years and then to decline by half until the middle of the century. The integration of agriculture with land and water management, and with ecosystem conservation is essential for both environmental sustainability and agricultural production.

An environmental perspective must guide the evaluation of all development projects, recognizing the role of natural resources in local livelihoods. This recognition must be informed by a comprehensive understanding of the perceptions and opinions of local people about their stakes in the resource base. To ensure the sustainability of the natural resource base, the recognition of all stakeholders in it and their roles in its protection and management is essential. There is need to establish well-defined and enforceable rights (including customary rights) and security of tenure, and to ensure equal access to land, water and other natural and biological resources. It should be ensured that this applies, in particular, to indigenous communities, women and other disadvantaged groups living in poverty.

Water governance arrangements should protect ecosystems and preserve or restore the ecological integrity of all natural water bodies and their catchments. This will maintain the wide range of ecological services that healthy ecosystems provide and the livelihoods that depend upon them. Biomass is, and will continue for a long time to be, a major source of fuel and energy, especially for the rural poor. Recognizing this fact, appropriate mechanisms must be evolved to make such consumption of biomass sustainable, through both resource management and the promotion of efficient and minimally polluting technologies, and technologies which will progressively reduce the pressures on biomass, which cause environmental degradation.

The traditional approaches to natural resource management such as sacred groves and ponds, water harvesting and management systems, etc., should be revived by creating institutional mechanisms which recapture the ecological wisdom and the spirit of community management inherent in those systems. All such environmental and ecological perspectives are taken into account in Mahatma Gandhi National Rural Employment Guarantee Act (MGNREGA).

This chapter attempts to examine and assess the environmental implications of the activities implemented under the MGNREGA. We undertook a rapid assessment of the environmental services provided by MGNREGA activities and their contribution towards reducing the vulnerability of production systems (for example, crop yields) and livelihoods to climate variability (for example, drought). The impact of activities has been analyzed through the two lenses of contemporary ecological science—environmental services and climate change.

5.2 MGNREGA: An Ecological Act

National Rural Employment Guarantee Act, 2005 provides for the enhancement of livelihood security of the households in rural areas of the country by providing at least one hundred days of guaranteed wage employment in every financial year to every household whose adult members volunteer to do unskilled manual work and for matters connected therewith or incidental thereto. This Act may be called the National Rural Employment Guarantee Act, 2005. The Act is a significant legislation in many ways. Unlike earlier employment schemes, it is demand-driven. People who need jobs will demand them, which the government is legally bound to provide. In case of failure to do so, the government has to dole out unemployment allowance.

For the first time, rural communities have been given not just a development programme, but also a regime of rights. The Act was preceded by three decades of attempts to bring in such a legislation. Simply put, the primary objective of the Act is 'enhancement of livelihood security in rural areas by providing 100 days of unskilled manual work' with the auxiliary objective being generating productive assets and protecting the environment. This Act is designed to provide an ecological perspective to the implementation of the programmes under the MGNREGA in order to achieve long-term livelihood sustainability. The ecological perspective is needed to work for the improvement of the natural resource base and for sustaining the ecological systems on which large number of people depend for their livelihoods.

An ecological act is one of the best features of the MGNREGA as it designates a balance between human action and natural resources creating a sustainable economic security through green jobs. The MGNREGA must be strengthened and revamped to provide not just wages for work done but work that will make ecological regeneration possible. MGNREGA has also been able to contribute to ecological restoration through its design. According to findings of a pilot study conducted by the Indian Institute of Science, Bangalore in Chitradurga district of Karnataka, there is an increase in groundwater level, increase in water percolation, and an improvement in soil fertility leading to improved land productivity. In addition to these findings, there has also been a reduction in water vulnerability and livelihood vulnerability in these areas.

The study also indicates that MGNREGA has some in-built limitations such as focus only on employment, activities not implemented according to a plan, spatially or time-wise, and disconnected and scattered implementation of activities, to name a few. But many of the MGNREGA activities still have the potential to provide environmental services, conserve and enhance natural resources (soil, water, and grass and forest resources). There is a need to identify such fail-proof activities that improve soil, water, grass and forest resources, even without micro-plans or watershed plans. Investment in MGNREGA activities, given the scale and importance, should lead to sustained flow of benefits such as employment, income, water supply, food and grass production. Such research suggests that MGNREGA works need to be seen as contributing to sustainable development. The successful implementation of the MGNREGA indicates that climate is conducive for a far-reaching, rights-based legislation to eliminate hunger and deprivation, sustainable environment and maintenance of ecosystem.

The activities under the MGNREGA are largely linked to water, soil and land, which are the key natural resources determining agricultural and livestock production. They can have a positive or negative influence on these natural resources, affecting their ability to provide environmental services. Environmental services include recharging groundwater, increasing rain water percolation, conserving water, increasing the area irrigated, reducing soil erosion, increasing soil fertility, conserving biodiversity, reclaiming degraded crop and grazing lands, enhancing the supply of leaf manure, fuel wood and non-wood forest produce, and carbon sequestration.

The goal of MGNREGA activities is to conserve natural resources and enhance environmental services to sustain food and livestock production, increasing the supply of fresh water for drinking, and increasing grass and forest product production. The benefits accruing from the activities implemented under the MGNREGA can be described as "services provided". The Millennium Ecosystem Assessment (MEA, 2005) considers humans as an integral component of the natural ecosystem unlike classical approaches, which differentiate humans as non-natural. The approach also addresses the sustainability of resources and livelihoods by considering human well-being a parallel theme to the functioning of the natural ecosystem.

5.3 Nature of Work under MGNREGA

Swaminathan, M.N. (2009) described MGNREGA as the world's largest ecological security and food security Act, which can successfully strengthen the ecological foundations for sustainable agriculture. By definition, food security involves every individual gaining physical, economic, social and environmental access to a balanced diet that includes the necessary macro- and micro-nutrients, safe drinking water, sanitation, environmental hygiene, primary healthcare and education so as to lead a healthy and productive life. The food should originate from efficient and environmentally benign production technologies that conserve and enhance the natural resource base of crops, farm animals, forestry, inland and marine fisheries. With the initiation of the MGNREGA, the minimum purchasing power for food security is being created in families living below the poverty line. Given the rising demand for food grains in future and irrigated areas having reached their plateau of productivity, development of rain-fed areas holds the key to future food security.

But India's rain-fed areas have been in the throes of an agrarian and unemployment crisis. That is the reason why the Act gives importance to agriculture and irrigation. Additionally, to meet this huge employment demand, it advocates productive use of the forestry sector for livelihood generation. The Act attempts to unlock the potential of the rural poor to contribute to the reconstruction of their environment. To achieve this, it has laid emphasis on creation of productive assets in villages. Out of nine preferred areas of works under the MGNREGA, seven focuses on water and soil conservation. The attention of the scheme is on the following works in their order of priority:

- Water conservation and water harvesting.
- Drought proofing (including afforestation and tree plantation).
- Irrigation canals (including micro and minor irrigation works).
- Provision of irrigation facility to land owned by households belonging to scheduled castes and scheduled tribes or to land of beneficiaries of land reforms or that of the beneficiaries under the Indira Awas Yojana of the Government of India.

- Renovation of traditional water bodies (including desilting of tanks).
- Land development.
- Flood control and protection works (including drainage in water-logged areas).
- Rural connectivity to provide all-weather access.
- Any other work, which may be notified by the Central government in consultation with the state government.

The priorities of the work to be undertaken include watershed management and water conservation, drought-proofing, flood protection, land development, minor irrigation and rural connectivity. Such work is important to strengthen the ecological foundations of sustainable agriculture. The MGNREGA is probably the world's largest ecological security programme, with the key provisions that investments in an employment guarantee programme must be in productive, eco-friendly assets. This would ensure that the resultant growth dynamic is both sustainable (by regenerating the environment) and non-inflationary (by easing the agrarian constraint). Not only does demand need stimulation, growth has to be sustainable in both economic and ecological terms, especially in these times of climate change.

For the nine years, since MGNREGA has been operational, the purpose of the Act was to create rural assets, important among them being water and soil conservation projects, especially minor irrigation works. Table 5.1 shows the various types of work undertaken through MGNREGA in the financial year 2014-15.

From Table 5.1, we can observe that all the work mentioned, would ensure the sustainability of ecology. The maximum number of work completed focused on rural connectivity with number at 60,664, followed by provision of irrigation facility to land owned at 57,810 and land development which was 50,054. The following table shows the total number of works completed during 2014-15 financial year (till August 31, 2014) under MGNREGA.

Table 5.1: Number of Works Completed during 2014-15 under MGNREGA

Focus on Work	2014-15*
Water Conservation and Water Harvesting	42,246
Flood Control and Protection	8,452
Drought Proofing	20,412
Micro Irrigation Works	9,498
Provision of Irrigation facility to Land Owned	57,810
Renovation of Traditional Water bodies	20,392
Rural Connectivity	60,664
Land Development	50,054
Any other activity approved by MRD	8,328

*as on 31.08.2014
Source: www.nrega.nic.in

5.4 MGNREGA and Environmental Services

Identifying the potential environmental services that result from MGNREGA activities is crucial to understanding and quantifying their impact on the ecology. The linkages and the trade-offs of interventions or changes in an ecosystem are very complex. The environmental services include the indicators which incorporate measurable physical, biological and socio-economic indicators, including livelihood indicators.

Global concerns related to food security, water security, adaptation to climate change and variability, and sustainable livelihoods have been given adequate importance. Indicators have been developed for assessing and quantifying the effect MGNREGA activities have on delivering these services. Services having direct implications within the ecological boundary of the activity and related components of the system are considered local. Village or micro-watershed boundaries have been considered local. Global services include those that have implications beyond regional boundaries (for example, climate change mitigation through carbon sequestration).

These indicators represent the indicators for poverty, environmental impact, socio-economic status, food security, fuel security, climate vulnerability and other aspects and are associated with several interlinked components of a village ecosystem (Table 5.2).

Table 5.2: MGNREGA Activities and Key Environmental Services: Local and Global

MGNREGA Activities	Local Environmental Services	Regional and Global Environmental Services
Water conservation and harvesting	Groundwater recharge, soil moisture retention and protection (erosion control), flood control (reduced risk), providing irrigation and drinking water and soil quality (nutrient cycling)	Water conservation
Irrigation provisioning and improvement	Providing irrigation, improved agriculture and livelihoods, increased crop production	—
Renovation of traditional water bodies	Improved storage capacity, irrigation availability, groundwater recharge, soil quality (nutrient cycling), biomass production and crop production	Water conservation
Land development	Land reclaimed for agriculture, improved–irrigation availability, hence agriculture and livelihood improvement	—
Drought proofing	Soil moisture retention, protection, (erosion control) and soil quality (nutrient cycling), flood control, (reduced risk), biomass production (fuel wood) and local climate regulation	Water conservation, carbon sequestration, biodiversity conservation
Flood control	Groundwater recharge, soil moisture retention and protection (erosion control) and flood control (reduced risk)	Water conservation

Source: www.nregaguidelines.nic.com

These environmental services result in the rise of the groundwater level, an increase in irrigated area and better soil fertility, thereby increasing food production, and contributing to water and food security in the villages. The environmental services include recharging shallow aquifers, increasing the water available for agriculture, and locally reducing soil erosion by trapping soil in check dams. The direct and major benefits of these structures will be arresting run-off rates and improving percolation. Thus, MGNREGA has the explicit potential to address both environmental and social concerns. In forested regions, this gives immense scope to design programmes for both livelihood security and resource sustainability. Thus, auxiliary objective of the Act is to strengthen natural resource management through works that address causes of chronic poverty like drought, deforestation and soil erosion and hence encourage sustainable development.

5.5 MGNREGA and Ecological Poverty

India is facing an adverse balance of poverty crisis as it generates more poverty than it eradicates. This explains the phenomenon of stagnating poverty. Excessive focus on conventional economic growth as an instrument of poverty alleviation has not worked. But one must understand that India's poverty is ecological poverty, unlike what conventional economists see as income poverty. India being a dominantly biomass-based society, ecological degradation triggers poverty here. The solution lies in regenerating the ecology with the people at the helm of the affairs. Healthy lands and ecosystems, when used in sustainable ways, can provide all the wealth that is needed for economically viable, healthy and dignified lives. For India to prosper, it needs to ensure sustainable livelihoods for its poor and mainstream the poor's experiences into national policies.

The challenge today lies in empowering and mobilizing people to enable them to escape from their 'ecological poverty', in order to create natural wealth, and develop a robust local economy. What is clear is that providing jobs in India demands a change in the way we do business. The formal industrial sector has never provided employment in this country. With greater mechanization in the years to come, its contribution towards generating employment is bound to decline further. The service economics—outsourcing included—will grow but cannot really absorb job seekers in a country like India. The key to generating employment lies in building productive and sustainable livelihoods based on natural resources. The potential is enormous—from planting trees for pulp to rearing animals for dairy farming; to rearing worms for silk and growing medicinal plants for pharmaceutical industries. It is critical that employment and enterprise go beyond the conventional economic opportunities.

There has also been a failure in understanding the real nature of employment in the country. Ecological assets like land and forests are the key employment sources for rural people in India. Any attempt to create employment must focus on these sectors. But our policies for employment generation have restricted themselves to employment *per se*, and completely ignored the fact that the generated employment opportunities need to be sustainable and allow the employed to move above the poverty line. Exclusive focus on the purely quantitative approach to employment generation has resulted in low quality of employment. The result: we do generate employment, but they become unproductive very soon, leaving people either unemployed once again or grossly underemployed.

The MGNREGA, with a focus on asset creation, attempts to be relevant to local needs. But it does not do enough to address the institutional and management gags that exist in the programmes of soil, water and forest conservation. These are fragile assets. They require management and maintenance. This is where the MGNREGA must be work on. The challenge is to use the Act to solve the problem of creating sustainable livelihoods through asset creation—facilitate the use of ecology for economy. The policy measures involve crucial changes in institutional, legal and financial frameworks, aimed at fashioning the programme into an opportunity for rural development.

The first aspect of the Act that could be relooked at is its evaluation and monitoring. Instead of the simple calculation on jobs demanded and provided, MGNREGA needs to be evaluated and monitored on its impact on livelihood security. Currently, the Union Ministry of Rural Development's national level monitors evaluate the Act on jobs creation and number of assets created under preferred works category. The real effectiveness of the scheme can be measured by using three parameters:

1. Increase in average annual income of households.
2. Increase in the productivity of small and marginal land holdings.
3. Quality and contribution of assets like water tanks.

By changing the evaluation parameters as suggested above, the scheme will assume the character of a rural development scheme, instead of a run-of-the-mill wage-earning programme. This will also help the government to ensure that most of the works taken up remain within the preferred works category, that is, productive assets.

Secondly, under the MGNREGA, as experiences in various states show, water conservation works are being taken up as stand-alone activities. Village ecology is a fragile combination of soil, water and forests. A water harvesting structure, for instance, is rendered useless if its catchment areas are left unprotected. Works under the scheme need to be planned in totality—to succeed; water conservation needs to take into account plantation works and drought proofing. The Second Administrative Reforms Commission has recommended that all works under the Act must be undertaken keeping in mind the overall improvement in total ecology.

5.6 MGNREGA and Decent Work in a Greener Economy

A green job is, according to the United Nations Environment Program, "work in agricultural, manufacturing, research and development (R&D), administrative, and service activities that contribute(s) substantially to preserving or restoring environmental quality. Green jobs are receiving unprecedented attention as signs of a more sustainable economy and a society that conserves the environment for present and future generations (ILO, 2008). The recent economic crisis has presented unique opportunities for moving towards a greener future by giving a major thrust to the forest sector that will generate employment, create real and durable assets and help rebuild rural India. Unemployment has been a serious problem in India since well before the recent economic crisis, and has been a major cause for political and social unrest.

Creating employment could also help resolve societal conflicts. Specifically, but not exclusively, this includes jobs that help to protect ecosystems and biodiversity; reduce energy, materials, and water consumption through high efficiency strategies; de-carbonize the economy; and minimize or altogether avoid generation of all forms of waste and pollution. Green jobs certainly include the direct employment which reduces environmental impact ultimately to levels that are sustainable. This includes jobs that help to reduce the consumption of energy and raw materials, decarbonizes the economy, protect and restore ecosystems and biodiversity and minimize the production of waste and pollution. Green jobs can lead to lower environmental impacts directly by reducing poverty. The range of profiles of green jobs stretches from highly skilled research and development or management functions through technical and skilled levels to the relatively low skilled ones. The largest numbers of already existing and future green jobs is concentrated in sectors directly linked to the use of energy and the recovery of raw materials, like:

- Improvements in energy efficiency, particularly in the building sector (renovation), but also industry and transport.
- Renewable energy.
- Mobility—mass transportation.
- Recycling and reuse.
- Sustainable use of natural resources—agriculture, forestry and fisheries.
- Environmental services.

Green growth and clean production are part of an overall drive towards production and consumption patterns which are compatible with sustainable development through transitions that take as a point of departure, the developmental needs of each country. It is one of the key challenges in the transformation to clean development to ensure that the green jobs associated with it are decent works and contribute to socially sustainable development. In addition to the employment potential, energy efficiency measures can contribute to poverty alleviation. Poor households tend to spend disproportionate share of their incomes on energy for electricity, heating and transport. Efficiency gains often translate into improvements in real incomes for the poor. MGNREGA is a good example of such a green job.

Green jobs under MGNREGA make it an exemplar model of adaptation to climate change. Evidence of the suitability of the choice of work in terms of ecological-contextual needs and its usefulness is emerging. There is a need to quantify the environment services of the rural poor rendered under this Act. Quantification of environmental services by the rural poor though green jobs that MGNREGA permits has been initiated on a pilot basis. This will not only assess the impact of MGNREGA works as an adaptation strategy to climate change, but they may also help build their case for co-benefits of environment services rendered through carbon credit. Such quantification studies need to be mainstreamed into regular programme tracking through appropriate institutional networks, at a regional level. Moreover, their methodologies and the lessons yielded should not be confined to academic debates but must be forged into instruments of community learning.

5.7 MGNREGA and Climate Change

Employment patterns and labour markets are in constant change driven by many factors including technology, trade, finance, demographics and as well as the environment. Maintaining a policy framework that facilitates and encourages change is one of the main responsibilities of employment and labour departments. Climate change and other environmental issues add a new dimension to that process of change which needs to be better understood so that policies and program can be well-tuned to meet the new challenges. MGNREGA can provide opportunity to face such issues and challenges. As discussed during the Copenhagen Climate Conference, it may be of interest to see how the National Rural Employment Guarantee Act, our most ambitious poverty reduction programme till date, fares with respect to climate change. MGNREGA links two of the most critical problems of our times, namely, extreme poverty and climate change.

The linkage is forged through environmental services which are provided by rural households when they engage in works under MGNREGA. Defined and prioritised under the Act, works can significantly change the environment through rejuvenation of the natural resource base. Water conservation, land development and afforestation through MGNREGA can provide local services such as groundwater recharge, enhanced soil fertility and increased biomass. These, in turn, can generate global benefits such as adaptation to and mitigation of climate change and biodiversity conservation.

While the primary objective of the Act is poverty alleviation, a further objective is stated, "...as creation of durable assets and strengthening the livelihoods base of the rural poor...". The livelihoods of the rural poor are directly dependent on environmental resources—land, water, forests—and are vulnerable to weather and climate variability—as water stress increases, groundwater levels recede, soil fertility declines and forest habitats disappear.

Climate change will only exacerbate the vulnerabilities of the rural poor. As climate-sensitive, natural ecosystems deteriorate, subsistence will slip further out of reach. India's rural poor, who have least contributed to it, will pay some of the problem's heaviest tolls. Thus, MGNREGA is to be designed to provide employment and income to the rural household, contributing directly to livelihood security, adversely affected by climate change.

5.8 MGNREGA and Ecological Infrastructure

In addition to supplementing wage employment, MGNREGA's secondary objective is to strengthen rural natural resource management. This is achieved by financing rural works that address causes of drought, deforestation and soil erosion, thus restoring the natural capital base on which rural livelihoods depend. As one of the world's leading crop producers, India has seen a surge in water consumption in the agriculture sector over the years. With industrial water consumption expected to quadruple between 2000 and 2050 as well, groundwater aquifers in the four major river basins may be depleted by half, by 2050. India is moving towards water scarcity due to increasing demand and a drop in supply of clean water as well, with forecasts of even a 50 percent deficit by 2030. Increasing water scarcity is a major constraint to agriculture and livestock production affecting livelihoods and food security.

Water conservation accounts for about half of the total projects supported under MGNREGA, with 850,000 water conservation works funded and completed from 2006 to 2008. For example, in the district of Jalaun (Uttar Pradesh), MGNREGA provided training and jobs for villagers to develop solutions to their heavily silted water harvesting infrastructure, alleviating their water shortage. In 2007-2008, more than 3,000 new soak pits, together with hand pumps were constructed. This has helped conserve an estimated 5 million litres of water. Similarly in Andhra Pradesh, MGNREGA supported the restoration of a network of water storage tanks dating back over 500 years in the principal arid zone. Repairs to the gates of the tanks, as well as works to desilt the channels feeding them, has been restored to full capacity. This not only boosts crop and livestock production but has contributed to groundwater replenishment also.

In its short history, MGNREGA has produced many such success stories across the country. In promoting inclusive growth and the restoration of ecological infrastructure, the programme also has a strong impact on empowerment of poor or marginalized groups. It has contributed to boosting the average wage for agricultural labourers since its inception.

5.9 Measures to Make MGNREGA More Eco-friendly

- Measures not only for the providing wages but also for asset creation. This will help in village development through productive asset creation.
- Give importance to forestation under MGNREGA by linking it to other forestry programmes.
- Conservation technologies—stress-tolerant, climate-resilient varieties of seeds, drip irrigation, zero-tillage, raised-bed planting, laser-levelling, systems of rice intensification (SRI)—can build adaptive capacities to cope with increasing water stress, providing "more crop per drop".
- Strengthening land development practices such as land levelling, conservation bench terracing, contour and graded bunding, and pasture development could prevent soil erosion and loss of organic matter. Reclamation of wastelands and degraded lands together with afforestation, horticulture plantation and agro-forestry have the potential to sequester carbon both above and below ground, thereby contributing to carbon mitigation.
- Creating green jobs through MGNREGA, thus enabling ecological security,
- Augmenting water resources.
- Enabling planned convergence with programmes of water resources, afforestation and agricultural productivity.
- Adaptive towards the adverse effects of climate change.
- If the nature of work relates to natural resource management, they contribute to enhancing the productivity of soil, augment water tables and increase vegetal cover.
- Labour intensive, green jobs are exemplar adaptation strategies for climate change. They combine economic advantages with environmental services.

The chapter validates that assets created under MGNREGA have been conducive to the geographical-ecological environment and have been useful and have contributed towards natural resource regeneration. The workers wanted to do something under MGNREGA to check soil erosion. Since MGNREGA is an ecological Act, it was suggested to set up a biological hedge that grows by the year and not degenerate like sea walls made of stone boulders. The Union Ministry of Rural Development has taken steps to achieve convergence of brain and brawn, by enlisting the support of Ministries and Departments. Such convergence of expertise for sustainable development will help to enhance farm productivity without causing ecological harm. There is also a need to raise the self-esteem of MGNREGA workers, making them feel proud of the fact that they are engaged in checking eco-destruction. Due recognition should be given to the MGNREGA groups that have done outstanding work in water harvesting, watershed development and soil healthcare with "Environment Saviour Awards". This will help spread awareness of the critical role MGNREGA workers play.

References

Centre for Science and Environment (2007), "An Ecological Act: A Backgrounder to the National Rural Employment Guarantee Act (NREGA)", *CSE*, New Delhi.

Centre for Science and Environment (2008), *The National Rural Employment Guarantee Act (NREGA): Opportunities and Challenges*, New Delhi.

Hirway, Indira (2005), "Enhancing Livelihood Security through National Employment Guarantee Act: Towards Effective Operationalization of the Act", *Indian Journal of Labour Economics*, Vol. 48, November 4, Ahmedabad: Centre for Development Alternatives.

http://cseindia.org/programme/nrml/nrml-index.htm.

ILO (2008), "Report on the National Workshop on Social Dialogue in the Water Sector in Kenya", (Nairobi, 26-27th November, 2007), Sectoral Activities Branch, ILO, Geneva.

Indian Institute of Science (2010), "Environmental Services,

Vulnerability Reduction and Natural Resource Conservation from MGNREGA Activities", Supported by *GIZ*.

Kareemulla, K., K. Srinivas Reddy and B. Venkateswarlu (2009), "Soil and Water Conservation Works through National Rural Employment Guarantee Scheme (NREGS) in Andhra Pradesh: An Analysis of Livelihood Impact", *Agricultural Economics Research Review*, 22, pp. 443-450.

Millennium Ecosystem Assessment (2005), *Ecosystems and Human Well-Being.*

Ministry of Rural Development, Government of India (2009), *National Rural Employment Guarantee Act*, New Delhi, India.

Ravindranath, N.H. and Rakesh Tiwari et al. (2009), "Environmental Services and Vulnerability Reduction through NREGA: Findings of the Rapid Assessment in Chitradurga District of Karnataka", Technical Report, *Centre for Sustainable Technologies,* Indian Institute of Science, Bangalore.

Reference Manual Ecological Considerations in Programme Implementation National Rural Employment Guarantee Programme (2007), Foundation for Ecological Security, *NDDB Campus*, Anand.

Rita Sharma (2009), "NREGA and Climate Change", *The Indian Express.*

Sharma, Ritika (2008), "NREGA: Impacts and Implementation Experiences: Poverty, Food Security and Environment", in *The National Rural Employment Guarantee Act (NREGA)-Design, Process and Impact,* New Delhi: Government of India, Ministry of Rural Development and UNDP.

Swaminathan. M.S. (2009), Synergy between Food Security Act and NREGA, *The Hindu*, June 1.

6

Millennium Development Goals (MDGs) and MGNREGA

6.1 Millennium Development Goals

Lack of satisfaction at the pace of human development in the 1980s inspired the United Nations to convene a series of global conferences in the 1990s to identify the problems involved and to commit the world community to addressing those problems. These World Summits set a series of goals, the Millennium Development Goals (MDGs), which has become the anchor around which international agencies have since tried to organize their developmental activities. The ongoing discussion on the modus operandi and the feasibility of achieving these targets has focused largely on the lack of resources. While resources are no doubt important, it is equally important to adopt the right kind of policies and institutions. This chapter argues that a well-designed employment policy will go a long way towards promoting some human development outcomes linked to the MDGs.

India is on course to move forward to achieve the targets of Millennium Development Goals which has accelerated its pace of poverty alleviation strategies by mobilizing greater budget resources, creating time frames for quantifiable deliverables, linking with global frameworks of action. Major strides have been made under the Mahatma Gandhi National Rural Employment Guarantee Act (MGNREGA)—a landmark legislation in India, which was enacted after a successful struggle for employment guarantee legislation. It has a direct connection with the efforts to accelerate the achievement of the MDGs in India; efforts are on towards total eradication of poverty by 2015. MGNREGA, with its rights based framework, is a paradigm shift from all other development programmes that were traditionally supply led. Centrally-funded entirely through domestic resources, the implementation of this Act is supported by a budget based on demand for employment. Apart from providing livelihood to millions of households, over the last nine years, the Act has become a significant vehicle for strengthening grassroot level democratic processes and regeneration of India's depleting natural resource base.

As part of poverty reduction efforts, India's Ministry of Rural Development emphasised that MGNREGA supports the achievement of three MDGs: Goal 1—eradicate extreme poverty and hunger; Goal 3—promote gender equality and empower women; and Goal 7—ensure environmental sustainability. The United Nations Global Assessment Report (GAR), praised MGNREGA as an endorsed employment programme and cash transfer to marginalized sections of the society as an important strategy that has the potential to reduce disaster risk and achieve the Millennium Development Goals and asked other nations to emulate the programme that has helped empower millions of marginalized.

6.2 Eradication of Hunger and Poverty

The first Millennium Development Goal (MDG) of 'eradicating extreme poverty and hunger' aims at reducing the proportion of people whose income is less than US$1 between 1990 and 2015, by half. These include, reducing the headcount ratio of consumption poverty by 10 percentage points, raising real wage rate of unskilled workers by 20 percent and creating 70 million new work opportunities. According to the National Sample Survey Organization, 300 million Indians live in extreme poverty. The estimates of Tendulkar Committee (2009) show that, between 1993-94 and 2003-04, aggregate poverty head count ratio of India has fallen only marginally from 45.3 percent to 37.2 percent. Similarly, the rural poverty has declined from 50.1 percent to 41.8 percent only and urban poverty has declined from 31.8 percent to 25.7 percent. These numbers convey that, out of every hundred rural people, around 42 people are still unable to get a decent livelihood.

There has been a "significant dent" in poverty in rural areas by increasing employment opportunities and proper wage disbursement through implementation of MGNREGA which has increased earning of rural households, resulting in an increase in their purchasing power. During the first year of implementation (2006-07) in 200 districts, 2.10 crore households were employed and 90.5 crore person days were generated. In 2007-08, 3.39 crore households were provided employment and 143.59 crore person days were generated in 330 districts. In 2008-09, 4.51 crore households were provided employment and 216.32 crore person days were generated across the country.

In 2013-14, 13.3 crore households were provided employment and 220.2 crore person days were generated.

6.3 Gender Equality and Empowerment of Women

The Employment Guarantee Act can also help to empower women, by giving them independent income-earning opportunities. MGNREGA provides that 30 percent of the employment provided, should be given to women. Implementation of MGNREGA has contributed to very high levels of women empowerment, particularly in the following aspects—that as the work is organized by women's groups, the gender perspective gets built in automatically, for the first time equal wages are really paid and this has boosted the earnings of women. As the bank deposits are increasing, the intra-household status of the women has also been improving commensurately as she controls substantial cash resources and withdrawal can be only on her decision. Women empowerment was not among the original intentions of the MGNREGA, and is not among its main objectives.

However, provisions like priority for women in the ratio of one-third of total workers [Schedule II (6)]; equal wages for men and women [Schedule II (34)]; and crèches for the children of women workers [Schedule II (28)] were made in the Act, with the view of ensuring that rural women benefit from the scheme in a certain manner. Provisions like work within a radius of five kilometres from the house, absence of supervisor and contractor, and flexibility in terms of choosing period and months of employment were not made exclusively for women, but have, nevertheless, been conducive for rural women.

Nevertheless, women have availed of the paid employment opportunity under MGNREGA in large numbers. Interestingly, this occurred largely spontaneously. Women's participation under MGNREGA, measured in person days, also exceeded their participation in erstwhile employment generation programmes like the Sampoorna Gramin Rojgar Yojana (SGRY) and the Maharashtra Employment Guarantee Scheme (MEGS). There are wide variations across states, within states and across districts in the share of work days for women. At the national level, the participation of women has increased significantly from 40.65 percent in 2006-07 to 47.92 percent in 2013-14.

The states like Kerala (92.95 percent) followed by Tamil Nadu (74.84 percent), Rajasthan (69.14 percent), marked high percent of women participation with lowest participation of states like Uttar Pradesh (19.39 percent) Assam (25.72 percent), Bihar (30.41 percent), West Bengal (33.21), during the financial year 2012-13. Participation of women has increased significantly. In several states, participation of women has surpassed men's participation, especially in Kerala and Tamil Nadu. Women perceived that MGNREGA is giving them a sense of independence and security.

Participation of women has increased significantly. In several states, participation of women has surpassed men's participation. In states of Kerala, the social organization like Kudumbashree is playing a critical role in the women participation which accounts for more than 90 percent of women and it became a "Women Program". In areas where rural women are traditionally homebound, such as Uttar

Pradesh, the Employment Guarantee Act has an even more significant role to play as a means of empowering rural women and curbing gender discrimination. Thus, it shows that the underprivileged majority is not completely marginalised in this elitist political system. With adequate political organisation, their demands can prevail over privileged interests.

6.4 MGNREGA and Restoration of Ecology

An ecological act is one of the best features of the MGNREGA, as it designates a balance between human action and natural resources thereby creating a sustainable economic security through green jobs and ensures the Millennium Development Goal of environmental sustainability. The MGNREGA must be strengthened and revamped to provide not just wages for work done but work that will make ecological regeneration possible. MGNREGA has also been able to contribute to ecological restoration through its design. The activities under the MGNREGA are largely linked to water, soil and land, which are the key natural resources determining agricultural and livestock production.

They can have a positive or negative influence on these natural resources, affecting their ability to provide environmental services. Environmental services include recharging groundwater, increasing rain water percolation, conserving water, increasing the area irrigated, reducing soil erosion, increasing soil fertility, conserving biodiversity, reclaiming degraded crop and grazing lands, enhancing the supply of leaf manure, fuel wood and non-wood forest produce and carbon sequestration.

The goal of MGNREGA activities has to be of conserving natural resources and enhancing environmental services to sustain food and livestock production, increasing the supply of fresh water for drinking, and increasing grass and forest product production. The benefits accruing from the activities implemented under the MGNREGA can be described as "services provided". The Millennium Ecosystem Assessment

(MEA, 2005) considers humans as an integral component of the natural ecosystem unlike classical approaches, which differentiate humans as non-natural. The approach also addresses the sustainability of resources and livelihoods by considering human well-being as a parallel theme to the functioning of the natural ecosystem. Out of nine preferred areas of works under the MGNREGA, seven focus on water and soil conservation.

The priorities of the work to be undertaken include watershed management and water conservation, drought-proofing, flood protection, land development, minor irrigation and rural connectivity. Such work is important to strengthen the ecological foundations of sustainable agriculture. The MGNREGA is probably the world's largest ecological security programme, with the key proviso that investments in an employment guarantee programme must be in productive, eco-friendly assets. This would ensure that the resultant growth dynamic is both sustainable (by regenerating the environment) and non-inflationary (by easing the agrarian constraint). Not only does demand need stimulation, growth has to be sustainable in both economic and ecological terms, especially in these times of climate change.

Ministry of Rural Development has taken steps to achieve convergence of brain and brawn, by enlisting the support of Ministries and departments. Such convergence of expertise for sustainable development will help to enhance farm productivity without causing ecological harm. There is also a need to raise the self-esteem of MGNREGA workers, making them feel proud of the fact that they are engaged in checking eco-destruction. Due recognition could be given to the MGNREGA groups that have done outstanding work in water harvesting, watershed development and soil healthcare with awards. This will help spread awareness of the critical role MGNREGA workers play.

MGNREGA is India's policy and programme commitment to achieve Millennium Development Goals and efforts are on towards total eradication of poverty by 2015. UNDP's network links and coordinates global and national efforts to reach these Goals. Although the year 2009, marked crossing of half-way point of MDGs, yet crucial development policies and finance are not systematically aligned with MDGs. As part of its poverty reduction mandate, UNDP is working to bridge this gap. UNDP is supporting a unique low cost ATM pilot initiative for MGNREGA implementation.

In addition, the Ministry of Rural Development and UNDP are in the process of piloting an IT initiative to link 200 district collectors virtually under the UN Country Team Solution Exchange Model. UNDP is in the process of commissioning up to 20 additional TV spots that document best practice implementation on MGNREGA from across the states and five major research institutions have been established to undertake a review of MGNREGA implementation and compliance.

References

Government of India, (2005), "Millennium Development Goals", Ministry of Statistics and Programme Implementation, *India Country Report.*

Millennium Ecosystem Assessment (2005), *Ecosystems and Human Well-Being,* UNDP.

Ministry of Rural Development, Government of India (2005), "The National Rural Employment Guarantee Act 2005 (NREGA): Operational Guidelines (2005)", New Delhi.

UNDP, "Human Development Report, 2003", Millennium Development Goals: A Compact among Nations to End Poverty, Oxford: Oxford University Press, 2003.

7

MGNREGA and Labour Migration

The non-availability of work in one's own village—either governmental or otherwise—is a condition which prompts migration. The non-relevance of the programmes, which are specially implemented to stop migration from a region, is also responsible for migration. For the landless and marginal farmers who are in constant debt, migration is the only choice for livelihood. The push arising out of lack of livelihood options in the village and indebtedness and crop loss leads to the pull factors such as the attraction of livelihood in the lean seasons.

However, it has been established that migration enables just enough earning to tide over the distress in the lean season and in no way helps to accumulate capital. There is a deep linkage between migration and poverty, especially of survival migration where women are found at the bottom of the pyramidal structure of poverty.

The phenomenon of migration is believed to have taken roots in the aftermath of severe drought of the 1960s. Today, every year thousands of people across the length and breadth of the country leave their native villages in search of food and employment. Most end up as bonded labourers being paid minimal daily wages. Alienation of land, labour and produce is the driving force for migration.

Though the migrants and their households might benefit than the individual, it is seen that this individual benefit occurs at the cost of net loss to both rural and urban areas, and a decline in social welfare, through overcrowding and increased population in urban destination areas and a greater regional concentration of wealth, income and human capital.

Traditionally, agriculture and related cottage industries were the only major professions in the rural areas. These professions could not absorb the ever increasing population in the rural areas. On the basis of a large sample survey in Bihar, Kerala and Uttar Pradesh, Oberai, Prasad and Sardana (1989) reported that in all the urban areas of the three states, female migrant work participation rates were generally higher among Christians and scheduled castes/tribes, whether married or unmarried. It was argued that availability of high productivity jobs in the rural areas could reduce in-migration to the urban areas. It is widely accepted that people move in search of employment and also from low wage to higher wage region—a rational choice to be able to earn more and improve their standard of living.

7.1 MGNREGA: An Alternative to Migration

The Mahatma Gandhi National Rural Employment Guarantee Act (MGNREGA) has been hailed as a landmark initiative to alleviate poverty and generate productive wage employment. This will also alleviate the problem of rural-urban migration. The Act on one hand can reap the rich human resources available in rural India to develop the most essential infrastructural facilities and on the other hand, can stem the migration of farmers/rural workers to cities. One of the significant objectives of MGNREGA is to arrest out-migration of unskilled, landless labour force from the rural areas to urban areas by ensuring up to 100 days of wage employment within their native jurisdiction so that the guaranteed wage employment can be judiciously and rationally utilized by the landless peasants during lean and distress seasons.

As far as possible, the work site should be within a five km. radius of the applicant's village—in case it is not, it must be provided within the block and the labourers must be paid 10 percent of their wages as extra wages to meet the additional travel and living expenses. This law can be a big boost for nomadic tribal communities, since locally domiciled but migrant population is also eligible for employment. The MGNREGA, too, could become a "predictable" source of local employment (since it guarantees work within a fortnight to anyone demanding it), and therefore reduces distress migration. In this respect, MGNREGA contrasts with previous employment programmes such as Jawahar Rozgar Yojana or Sampoorna Grameen Rozgar Yojana.

According to the Tenth Five Year Plan (2002-2007), "The Wage employment programmes, an important component of the anti-poverty strategy, have sought to achieve multiple objectives. They not only provide employment opportunities during lean agricultural seasons but also in times of floods, droughts and other natural calamities. They create rural infrastructure, which support further economic activity. These programmes also put an upward pressure on market wage rates by attracting people to public works programmes, thereby reducing migration".

The MGNREGA will have a significant positive impact on seasonal rural-urban migrations by providing rural workers with employment during the lean season. This will reduce the problems of excessive population pressure in urban Indian cities as surplus rural labour will find employment in their own villages. The MGNREGA will also have an impact on permanent migrations trends. While it is difficult to ascertain what the exact impact will be, one can assume that the improved infrastructure and increased activity in the rural economy due to increased purchasing power will lead to higher rates of permanent job creation, thus mitigating the urgency to migrate. Before MGNREGA, the tribal villagers had no option but to move from place to place during off-fishing/off-agricultural season. But with employment guarantee scheme in place, they have a source of livelihood during drought and off-fishing seasons. The lack of exact official data on migration is a matter that should be corrected as soon as possible as it is quite important to quantify this as accurately as possible as rural-urban migration can become quite a problem for both the source and the destination areas.

7.2 Studies on Migration

Although it is too early to judge or assess the programme, our investigations highlight some other important trends. There are so many studies related to the effect of MGNREGS on migration which generally show a decreasing trend—some of them are follows.

- A study conducted by Kartik Bhatia and Ashish Ranjan (2009) shows that more than half (57 percent) of the sample workers stated that the MGNREGA "helped them avoid migration", and a similar proportion (also 57 percent) felt that migration had decreased in their villages after the MGNREGA was launched. As expected, these figures were even larger in areas with high levels of MGNREGA employment or high rates of migration before the inception of the programme. For instance, in Pati block (Madhya Pradesh), a hub of out-migration where the MGNREGA has been deployed in a big way, 92 percent of the sample workers felt that migration had gone down and 88 percent said the MGNREGA had helped them avoid migration.
- According to R.D. Maurya and Gadkar (2006), the recognized researchers on migration at the Ambedkar Institute of Social Research, opined that MGNREGS has reduced migration by 15-20 percent in some villages of Mandla, Jhabua, Dhar and Dindori. Field level observations showed that this reduction was seen especially in the case of women and families with more than one or two male adult workers who stay behind in the expectation that they will get work locally. The scheme has improved the bargaining power of migrants by tightening the labour market and pushing up the wages.
- A study by Dreze and colleagues (2009) showed that NREGA helped to avoid migration by 59 percent and sending children to school by 38 percent. Rural-urban

migration leads to a misallocation of labour between rural and urban sectors in the sense that it raises urban unemployment, underemployment and poverty.

- Narayan Chandra Nayak et al. (2011), in their study of Mayurbhanj and Balasore District in Odisha revealed that on an average, about 69 percent of the respondents had reported that there has been an acceleration in employment opportunities on account of the MGNREGS and about 54 percent had said that migration has come down in the aftermath of implementation of the Scheme. This clearly indicates that before the introduction of MGNREGS, people in Mayurbhanj had limited livelihood opportunities forcing them to migrate outside on a large scale and the scheme has been able to solve these problems considerably. It may thus be said that MGNREGS has been successful in meeting its set objectives on this vital front. The outcome is equally better across education levels and age groups.

7.3 Cost of Migration

In explaining migration across space, according to Harris and Todaro (1970), income differentials are taken as the motivating factors in moving people from low-income areas to relatively high-income areas. Even though in urban areas, expected wage rate is higher than the rural wage rate, people are reluctant to migrate because of the cost of migration that hampers it. The willingness to accept a lower wage in the village reflects the cost of migration as well as the exploitative conditions that labourers face as migrants. Emergence of studies by Dreze and Khera, and by Indian School of Women's Studies and Development, highlight that MGNREGA has indeed led to a decrease in distress migration from village, with workers stating that the preference to work in and around the villages, rather than bearing social and other costs of migrating elsewhere in search of work. The costs of migration include transport costs, uncertain earnings, health hazards, and higher costs of living in urban areas combined with poor living conditions—they do not have the connections to settle down in an urban area, where rents are high and the area itself would be quite unfamiliar and they face a high risk because there is no guarantee that they will be employed throughout the year.

Migration also results in a breakdown of social life. This is true both in the case of men migrating alone and when entire families migrate. When entire families migrate, the situation is even worse—children have to be removed from schools and they live in precarious environments.

Women and young girls are especially vulnerable to sexual exploitation. Further, urban congestion is a cost of migration that is borne by the society at large.

Thus, MGNREGA has led to a decrease in migration from villages—with given preference to work in and around their villages, rather than bearing the social and other costs of migrating elsewhere in search of work—because it provides stable, certain and predictable employment within the five kilometres radius which provides a unique opportunity to protect people from these hardships.

7.4 Migration and Education

The villagers tend to migrate along with their families in hope that they might be able to employ their children in cities. This is not only exposing the children to the hazards of child labour but also leading to children dropping out of school during the academic year which shows how migration was directly connected to lack of education among children. Field visits done by Neera Burra (2008) in the villages of Dungarpur district to study the incidence of child migrant labour were extremely revealing which is notorious for large-scale migration of children between the age group of 10 to 14 to work in the BT cotton fields in Gujarat. Children also migrate to Gujarat to work in brick kilns, in *dhabas*, in workshops, in textile markets and on construction sites. Discussions with villagers revealed that there has been almost a 20 percent reduction in the incidence of migration amongst children which shows a reduction in child labour as a direct result of the impact of MGNREGA. People did say that if there were residential schools for 10-14 year old children, then more parents would keep their children in school.

It was found that some of the villagers spent their MGNREGA income to improve the quality of education of their children by paying the admission fee, purchasing books, providing tuitions, buying school uniforms, bicycle etc. Due to the construction of a connecting road, children got better connectivity to go to school by bicycle or on foot and now, children are more regular in terms of attending the school. There is a clear tendency of using the additional wage income for the education of children. It builds a case of inherent demand for children's better education. Most of the MGNREGA benefited families utilized their income for accessing children's education or supplementing with additional facilities to improve the quality of education. This long-term investment of MGNREGA wage income will further strengthen the capacity of the families for their upward mobility. Thus, reduction in the migration of both adults and children and an increased enrolment and retention of children in schools were the major impacts of MGNREGA, according to the villagers. Surely, even the critics of MGNREGA would agree that these are worthwhile goals for a sound public policy.

7.5 Effect of Migration on Agriculture

MGNREGA income in wages has two dimensions. The families owning small agricultural land which is insufficient to generate food security for the whole of the year or create additional surplus of cash to meet other basic needs helps families supplement their agricultural income with wage income of MGNREGA. There are large number of small land holding families having low agricultural produce; MGNREGA income provides a significant value addition to meet their higher order needs critical for their survival, growth and development of their family. There are families who are completely landless and depend on wage labour or look for work in agriculture sector or civil works. In the off-season for agriculture, such families migrate to towns. Civil works started in villages has given them options to earn in the village even if the wage rates are lower in the MGNREGA civil works. Even if the younger family members migrate as skilled labourers, middle aged unskilled family members prefer to stay in the village and work under MGNREGA.

This apart, the guaranteed employment under MGNREGA has restrained the usual seasonal labour migration, which has become the mainstay of farming in agriculturally progressive, but labour-starved states. This has caused acute shortage of labour for agriculture. It has particularly affected plantations in the southern states, notably Kerala and Punjab and the cultivation of labour-intensive crops like rice, wheat and sugarcane. The farmers are forced to incur additional expenses for using machines and energy for doing farm operations which were earlier performed manually by migratory labour at far lower costs. Sale of tractors and crop sowing and harvesting machines is reported to have risen sharply as a result of this. Farmers' organizations have come out with a sensible suggestion that the mandatory 100 days employment in a year should be provided only during agriculturally lean seasons. This will be a win-win situation for both farmers and the farm labour. While the farmers will get labour when they need it the most, the labourers will be able to remain employed for a longer period in a year. Although increased wage rate has reduced distressed migration from rural to urban areas substantially, it has adversely affected the availability of labour in the agricultural fields of many states where wages were very low before the introduction of MGNREGA.

7.6 Social and Economic Implications of Reduced Migration

World Development Report (2009) welcomed and encouraged the process of migration arguing that globally as well nationally, people move in order to improve their prospects in life. Negative attitudes held by government and ignorance of the benefits of population mobility has caused migration to be overlooked as a force in economic development. This contradicts India's policy of countering migration by setting up industries in backward areas and offering temporary employment through schemes like the National Rural Employment Guarantee Programme.

While this seems to be socially desirable, this emphasis on reducing migration *per se* is problematic. The evidence shows that it is likely that migration will continue or even increase with development as enhanced resources become available and access improves. Pattern of migration may change, but mobility is clearly the part of development path of a society.

Further, it is critical to take into account that migration tends to be a part of established livelihood strategies of household; which they are likely to give up easily and public policy should focus on supporting these strategies rather than on trying to minimize them for optimal outcomes.

Rather, policies that try to reduce the exploitation of migrants should be based on an understanding of the complexity of migration pattern, motives and outcomes and should take into account the perspectives of migration.

Although there has been some decline in the incidences of migration from the beneficiary households, seasonal and distressed migration continues to take place. This is primarily because of the non-availability of jobs when needed, and the lack of awareness about the details of the provisions and entitlements under the Scheme among the potential beneficiaries of the Scheme. The efforts to educate these migrants about the benefits of the MGNREGS at the place of departure itself is likely to have an impact and persuade the migrants to stay back in their home states and avail benefits of this Scheme. The aspect of MGNREGA where it can be used to curb rural-urban migration is conditional on that it is being implemented well in that region, otherwise, if work is not supplied, if wages aren't paid on time and if money is just being siphoned-off, then workers will have no incentive to stay back and would consequently migrate.

However, it should be clear that the primary aim of the Act is to provide welfare to the section of population that does not even earn the minimum wages—the fact that it can also curb distress migration, is just a positive secondary impact of the Act. It may be suggested here that the focus of the Act should be to prevent rural-urban migration which could really have a positive impact on economic development.

References

Centre for Science and Environment (2008), *National Employment Guarantee Act (NREGA): Opportunities and Challenges*, Natural Resource Management and Livelihood Unit, New Delhi.

Bhatia, Kartika and Ashish Ranjan (2009), "Alternative to Migration", *Frontline*, Vol. 26, Issue 1, January 3-16.

Burra, Neera (2008), "NREGA and its Impact on Child Labour: Field Notes from *Dungarpur*".

Dreze, Jean and Khera, Reetika (2009), "The Battle for Employment Guarantee", *Frontline*, 26 (01), January 3-16.

Haan de Arjan (2011), "Inclusive Growth? Labour Migration and Poverty in India", *The Indian Journal of Labour Economics*, Vol. 54, No. 3, July-September.

Harris, J., and M.P. Todaro (1970), "Migration, Unemployment and Development: A Two Sector Analysis", *American Economic Review* 60:126-42.

Jacob, Naomi (2008), "The Impact of NREGA on Rural-Urban Migration: Field Survey of Villupuram District, Tamil Nadu", *Summer Research Internship Programme, Centre for Civil Society.*

Maurya, R.D. and Gadkar (2006), "Migration: Labour Flows and Capital Transfers", *Ambedkar Institute of Social Research.*

Ministry of Rural Development, Government of India (2005), *The National Rural Employment Guarantee Act 2005 (NREGA): Operational Guidelines*", New Delhi.

Nayak, Narayan Chandra et al. (2011), "Appraisal of Processes and Procedures of NREGS in Orissa: A Study of Mayurbhanj and Balasore District", Department of Humanities and Social Sciences, Indian Institute of Technology, Kharagpur.

Oberoi, A.S., Pradhan, H. Prasad and M.G. Sardana (1989), "Determinants and Consequences of Internal Migration in India: Studies in Bihar, Kerala and Uttar Pradesh", Delhi: Oxford University Press.

Planning Commission, Government of India (2008), *Eleventh Five Year Plan (2007-2012), Volume-1: Inclusive Growth,* Oxford University Press, New Delhi.

UNDP (2009), *Human Development Report, 2009,* Reshaping Economic Geography, Palgrave Macmillan, Basingstoke.

8

Budgetary Allocation and its Utilization under MGNREGA

MGNREGA has been revolutionary in its promise of inclusive growth and financial inclusion, the right to work, the dignity of labour and a rational, participatory relationship with the state which provides at least one hundred days of guaranteed wage employment in a financial year to every rural household whose adult members volunteer to do unskilled manual work.

In providing basic wage security, the scheme provides a social safety net for India's most vulnerable households, providing an impetus for the development of a vibrant agricultural economy. MGNREGA was introduced in 200 of the country's most backward districts in 2006, extended to 130 more districts in 2007, and expanded to cover the entire country in 2008 with the exception of those districts that have 100 percent urban population. The government has referred to it as an *"Act of the people, by the people, and for the people"*.

The 'right to work' is a 'directive principle' in Indian Constitution which was formalized through the enactment of MGNREGA. It is seen as a mechanism of income transfer, infrastructure development and promoting rural production and consumption—a multifarious strategy indeed. MGNREGA is unique—being large in size, it intends to cover long periods, disburse huge funds and be dynamically responsive to climatic and rainfall conditions and above all open to any adult intending to work for wages often lower than local causal wages. Since self-targeting is inherent to the scheme—besides chronic poverty, manifest in food inadequacy—it also intends to mitigate idiosyncratic risks and shocks faced by households due to being differently-abled or death of an earning member. This chapter, based on the budgetary allocation of MGNREGA and the use of funds released under the MGNREGA by the central government, examines the budgetary incidence, financial issues and spatial dimension of the progress of implementation of the Act across states in India.

8.1 Budgetary Allocation and Fiscal Concern

The finance forms the most critical input for every programme's implementation—in order to grow and survive. Though the Act has been passed and implemented, the issue that remains pertinent is the implications of such a large and open-ended commitment for managing the revenue and fiscal deficits, especially in the context of the obligations under the Fiscal Responsibility and Budget Management Act. Before formalizing the Act, government agencies estimated that full coverage of MGNREGA will cost ₹ 400 billion (about US$ 9-10 billion) which was about 1 percent of the country's GDP. Some empirical assessments suggest that MGNREGA could help reduce rural poverty to 23 percent during the lean season, at an annual cost of 1.7 percent of GDP. Others based on simple average minimum wage aggregates of all states, estimated the national annual cost to be 1.3 percent of the GDP; and a case was made that MGNREGA will be sensitive to prevailing minimum wages in respective states.

Earlier wage employment programmes that sought to guarantee were constrained by the lack of budget funds, and, so instead of a legal guarantee, assurances alone were offered. It is possible that the confidence of the government to commit funds was inspired by a higher growth rate of the economy; but the significant point here is that even when the economy slowed down as a result of the global meltdown, the budgetary support to MGNREGA did not decline. Government of India releases the fund through budgetary policies for financing and implementation of this programme. Table 8.1 shows the budgetary allocation of funds, reflecting a steady increase from ₹ 11,300 crore in 2006-07 to ₹ 40,100 crore in 2010-11.

However, in the following years, the budgetary allocation has come down which, of course, will adversely affect the implementation of the MGNREGA.

Table 8.1: Financial Allocation of MGNREGA

Year	Budget Alloca-tion (₹ crore)	% of GDP	M Exp. as % of Total Exp.	M Exp. as % of Revenue Receipts	M Exp. as % of Fiscal Deficit	M Exp. as % of Rural Develop-ment
2006-07	11,300	0.28	1.2	1.6	6.10	46.55
2007-08	12,000	0.26	1.5	1.9	10.0	41.71
2008-09	30,000	0.56	1.6	2.0	10.8	52.77
2009-10	39,100	0.66	2.7	4.4	9.21	69.08
2010-11	40,100	0.54	2.8	4.1	9.01	55.63
2011-12	40,000	1.02	3.1	5.0	9.70	53.98
2012-13	33,000	0.78	2.2	3.0	6.42	33.33
2013-14	33,000	0.88	1.98	3.12	6.08	41.15

M = MGNREGA

Source: Budget Documents, Government of India.

It certainly indicates that the government seeks to cap the rural employment programme at this level. Otherwise, those who have worked for more than 15 days during the preceding financial year under the MGNREGA have been extended the Rashtriya Swasthya Bima Yojana (RSBY) under the budget which will benefit the below poverty line workers and their families in rural areas. But one of the biggest surprises in the 2011-2012 budget was that spending on the country's landmark rural employment program remained flat, disappointing activists who see it as a way of redressing growing wealth disparities. The year 2012-13 and 2013-14 budgets also show a declining budgetary allocation (₹ 33,000 crore) and this may not be able to contribute to growing employment demand under MGNREGA.

The funding of MGNREGA has been carved out by amalgamating all past programmes and it still constitutes just about 40-50 percent of the annual budgetary allocation of the Department of Rural Development, Government of India. It stipulates that the respective states have to contribute 25 percent of the cost of wages and materials used during the programme implementation.

The budgetary support to wage employment programmes before MGNREGA, was the highest in the year 2005-2006 when SGRY and NFFWP were under implementation—SGRY in all the districts and NFFWP along with it in 150 districts of the country.

The Maharashtra EGS, for about the last three decades, followed a different funding model entirely supported by the state legislative body, which continued to raise its (the state's) share of funds for MGNREGA by imposing (state) tax specifically for this purpose. Whether the current MGNREGA cost sharing between the Centre and the States is feasible or not, depends upon a number of factors including the state-level political will, public demand, and the fiscal prudence of the state governments. At the national level, MGNREGA allocation and expenditure hovers between 2-3 percent of the central (revenue account) outlays for the past few years. Any further expansion of MGNREGA in terms of a deepening of the programme need not be a cause for concern with respect to its adverse impact on the national level fiscal deficit, even if no additional tax or levy in the name of MGNREGA is imposed. Due to the economic slowdown during the last two quarters of the financial year 2008-09 and the expected continuation, one can expect a strain on country's fiscal deficit and therefore on MGNREGA allocations as well.

One of the greatest fears as regards the MGNREGA is its burden on the exchequer. It is believed that government will find ways of containing the expenditure by complicating the application procedures, in spite of the formal legal guarantee. This is what has happened in Maharashtra, where the cost of Employment Guarantee Scheme has been driven down to barely 0.2 percent of state domestic product. Even if the government in full spirit implements MGNREGA, the expenditure incurred is not expected to be futile. Expenditure may be incurred on infrastructure development activities, which would generate substantial secondary benefits even years after the completion of the work. Well-designed workfare programmes under the MGNREGA will construct much-needed infrastructure and thus minimize the trade-off between public spending on income transfers versus public spending on development. Also, all existing rural-development/poverty-alleviation schemes will be brought under the umbrella of the MGNREGA. Thus, while expenditure will be incurred on the scheme in an accounting sense, in reality, there may be a trivial increase in the share of the budget actually being spent on rural development/poverty alleviation.

8.2 Financial Performance

The Act stipulates that while implementing the projects, labour cost and material cost should be in the ratio 60:40. This ratio should be applied preferably at the *gram panchayat*, block and district levels. For smooth implementation, the engineer is required by the law to visit the work site at least once in two weeks and the overseer is to visit every day. In spite of these guidelines, the overseer do not visit the work site as stipulated, and the visits of the engineers are also very few and far in between. Tools and implements should be procured to enable the workers to execute the work. The cost of tools and implements may be booked under the material component of the project. State governments should devise a mechanism for transparent method of procurement of materials to be used under MGNREGA.

The Central Government provides funds for the wages and for ¾th of the material costs. The State Government pays for ¼th of the material costs. The actual percent of expenditure on wages, material and other administrative heads in various years is shown in Table 8.2.

Table: 8.2: Utilization of Funds under MGNREGA (in percent)

Year	Expenditure on Wages	Expenditure on Material	Administrative Expenditure
2006-07	66.21	30.89	2.09
2007-08	68.54	30.58	3.12
2008-09	69.27	30.08	3.48
2009-10	69.77	30.23	3.29
2010-11	68.36	31.64	4.57
2011-12	76.39	23.61	3.69
2012-13	75.30	24.71	4.56
Mean	70.55	28.82	3.54

Source: www.nrega.nic.in

If we look at Table 8.2, one can observe that the percentage of MGNREGA funds on wages is higher than the defined ratio. The share of expenditure on wages has increased from 66.21 percent in 2006-07 to 75.30 percent in 2012-13, while the share of expenditure on material has reduced and expenditure on administration of MGNREGA has also shown a slight variation. The expense on wages (skilled and unskilled), material and administration in different states shows the same trend. The mean expenditure on wages is 70.55 percent during the given period. In major states where data was available, the payment on wages was nearly 70 percent, and that on material was around 30 percent. The other contingency expenses were around 1 percent, except in the case of Uttar Pradesh, where contingency expenses were slightly above 2 percent.

8.3 State Expenditures and Household Wage Accruals

A state-wise break-up of utilization shows that while most states managed to utilize over 55-60 percent of allocated funds, some states like Maharashtra, Jammu and Kashmir, and Arunachal Pradesh among others, have used less than 50 percent of the allocated funds. Data from the Ministry of Rural Development shows that funds utilisation by Assam had improved by 200 percent, while Maharashtra's utilisation had risen by 60 percent. A look at the total expenditures suggests that Madhya Pradesh, Andhra Pradesh and Rajasthan have distributed ₹ 10-17 billion as wage payments followed by Uttar Pradesh, Chhattisgarh, West Bengal and Bihar, with the utilized amounts ranging between ₹ 5 and ₹ 10 billion each.

Three states had sought more funds under the government's rural employment scheme to meet a surge in demand for jobs from farm hands affected by fluctuation in monsoon rains. Poor rainfall in Maharashtra, Jharkhand and Assam had dried up the farm work, compelling farm workers to turn to MGNREGA. Enrolments under MGNREGA, initiated primarily to ensure livelihood in lean farm seasons, are usually low during monsoons, which overlaps with the peak farm season. But with more job seekers, these states have overshot their estimates of work demand under MGNREGA forcing them to seek more funds from the Centre. Rainfall has not been that good in some areas and some of the states had come together for an upward revision in the initial estimates.

8.4 Financial Implementation Issues

It is also surprising to find that this scheme has not been able to provide the employment that one would have expected in poor states—which is largely to do with the implementation and funding. The MGNREGA provides for a multi-tier structure of authority for implementation and monitoring of the scheme with specified functions and duties for each authority. Although there are various agencies involved for implementation of the scheme, the *gram panchayat* is responsible for all other works related to planning and implementation. The responsibility of the *gram panchayat* is the identification, execution and supervision of projects as per the recommendations of *gram sabha* (village assembly).

For accountability and transparency purposes, the *gram sabha* is given the powers to conduct a regular social audit of the individual schemes. The authority entrusted with the implementation as laid down, indicates that a coordinated approach of different tiers of governments or vertical coordination is critical for successful implementation of the scheme. Also, the horizontal coordination across departments for programme identification and execution of work through the panchayat assumes critical importance. These do not seem to be working too well.

As specified in the Act, for the purpose of funding and the implementation of the Scheme, the Central government will set up a National Employment Guarantee Fund. Individual state governments will also set up their State Employment Guarantee Fund to make a matching contribution under the Scheme. The funding pattern as laid down in the Act specifies that the centre's obligation would be to bear the cost on the items which includes the entire cost of wages of unskilled manual workers, 75 percent of the cost of material and administrative expenses as may be determined by the Central government, which will include *inter alia*, the salary and the allowances of the programme officer and the supporting staff at the work site facilities and expenses of the National Employment Guarantee Council.

The state governments' share would include 25 percent of the cost of material and wages of skilled and semi-skilled workers, unemployment allowance payable in case the state government cannot provide wage employment on time, administrative expenses of the State Employment Guarantee Council and administrative expenses towards salary of the officials at district and state levels appointed under MGNREGA.

It has been specified in the Act that "if an applicant under this Act is not provided such employment within 15 days of his application seeking employment", he shall be entitled to a daily unemployment allowance which will be paid by the state government. This implies an inbuilt structure of incentive for performance and disincentive for non-performance for the state government, as the inability to provide employment would require the state government to pay an unemployment allowance for which there is no contribution from the Centre. In other words, individual states will have to evolve a well-coordinated approach to equate supply of employment in accordance with the demand.

While MGNREGA is a Centrally-sponsored scheme, administratively managed by the Ministry of Rural Development, its implementation is exclusively done by the respective state government. The states are expected to systematically make a claim over the allocated resources by planning MGNREGA work activities and turning them into projects. An accumulation of such projects is used to appropriate funds from the scheme resources earmarked through a budgetary process. Often, the states are unable to execute the programme efficiently due to the shortage of administrative and implementing personnel at the grassroots level and sometimes due to inter-party political differences—the party in power in the concerned state is different from the one ruling at the Centre.

This becomes all the more important, as there is no supply side selection of beneficiaries. It requires an in depth understanding of region-specific labour demand and its seasonality so that a demand-based scheme of projects can be implemented at a frequency matching the demand for work instead of relying on supply side provisioning. Failure to fulfil these requirements may result in an imprudent use of funds, as the inability to provide employment on demand will impose the burden of compensation in the form of unemployment allowance on the state government.

Thus, there is a need to design a monitoring mechanism by strengthening the institutional structure at the local level so that resources can be used optimally. As it is a demand-based provisioning system, the flow of resources from higher levels of the government to the *panchayats* needs to be assured according to the demand. Thus, it is necessary to evolve a clear mechanism for flow of funds as needed, according to the demand rather than through the normal bureaucratic procedures. This would also require coordination between providing work and the provisioning of funding. Stringent conditionalities in funds release apart, the demand-based provisioning may be potentially regressive. As it stands now, under the scheme, funds will be released based on the annual work plan and budget proposal of the respective states.

A unique and radical programme, MGNREGA requires time, to be fully or even substantially streamlined. Unfortunately, there is a sense of nervousness in the bureaucracy about increasing expenditure that has resulted in a narrow and parsimonious scheme. Funding was argued by Jean Dreze and others to be possible through improved tax administration and reforms, yet the tax-GDP ratio has actually been falling. The main characteristic of the Scheme is sluggish with low spending, rather than checking wastage and 'leakages'. The bureaucracy seems to be in the grips of some kind of fear and lethargy, or simply a resistance to disturbing the pre-existing power equations at the local level. This stems from pessimism of the developmental outcomes of this programme, suspicion surrounding its empowerment spin-off and changing balance of power and an overall climate of fiscal tightening and low spending.

9

MGNREGA and Good Governance

In two general elections since 2004, the "other" India has spoken loud and clear to the few enclaves of prosperity that dot the country's grim development landscape: if growth is not inclusive and broad-based, its wheels will come off, severely undermining the very fabric of Indian democracy. Government of India has accelerated its pace of poverty alleviation strategies by mobilizing greater budget resources, creating timeframes for quantifiable deliverables, linking, with global frameworks of action, such as the Millennium Development Goals which provide an umbrella approach for addressing multi-dimensional deprivations. As a democratic country, a central feature of good governance is the constitutionally protected right to elect government at various levels in a fair manner, with effective participation by all sections of the population.

9.1 Uniqueness of MGNREGA

The seriousness and urgency of these policy and resource commitments to poverty alleviation are exemplified in a single legislation, National Rural Employment Guarantee Act (NREGA) which enacted on August 23, 2005 and got presidential assent on September 5, 2005 and is one of the largest and most ambitious anti-poverty schemes which will strengthen livelihood security through time bound guaranteed wage employment and is a paradigm shift from all other development programmes that were traditionally supply-led. Centrally-funded entirely through domestic resources, the implementation of this Scheme is supported by a budget based on demand for employment. It was "an Act to provide for the enhancement of livelihood security of the households in rural areas of the country by providing at least one hundred days of guaranteed wage employment in every financial year to every household whose adult members' volunteer to do unskilled manual work and for matters connected or incidental thereto" (NREGA, 2005).

Besides employment generation, the objective of the Scheme is to create durable community assets for strengthening of the livelihood source on a sustainable basis. It serves as a social safety net by providing a source of employment—as such it is an "employer of last resort". It was initially called the National Rural Employment Guarantee Scheme (NREGS) but was renamed on October 2, 2009 as Mahatma Gandhi National Rural Employment Guarantee Scheme (MGNREGA). The other key attributes of this Scheme are time bound guarantee, labour-intensive work, decentralized participatory planning, women empowerment, work site facilities, and above all, transparency and accountability through the provision of social audits and right to information. The process outcome of this Act is creating a model of governance reform anchored on the principles of right to livelihood, transparency and grassroot democracy.

However, much more needs to be done before MGNREGA possibilities become a reality. The record of productive assets creation has been poor if not altogether dismal. Long delays in wage payments—sometimes for several months—and the spectre of corruption rearing its ugly head indicate the failure of entitlements reaching the poorest of the nation, thus defeating the very purpose of MGNREGA. An analysis of these symptoms suggests that there are clear reasons why the results are not along the expected lines. Though no magic bullet or quick fixes exist, solutions may well be within our reach. As several observers have remarked, a critical lacuna in the implementation of MGNREGA has been the shortage of dedicated human resource, with an overloaded bureaucratic structure given "additional charge", leading to delays and poor quality output.

Attempts to piggyback a radically new people-centred

programme on to a moribund bureaucratic structure of implementation, simply do not work. However, a dedicated implementation structure will only solve part of the problem. The second crucial missing link in the implementation chain is concurrent monitoring. Here, information technology (IT) has a huge role to play in making necessary information available transparently and at high speed. Rich though, the MGNREGA management information system (MIS) is, there is much scope for improvement. The MIS, for instance, is not able to raise an alert on delays in wage payments because data are normally updated post-facto, thus undermining the very basis of monitoring.

MGNREGA is a unique and unprecedented effort in strengthening grassroot democracy in India. For the first time, the Indian state has legally mandated the implementation of mechanism that strengthens transparency and accountability at every step of the delivery chain, by creating platform for citizens to articulate their voice and directly engage with the state. This legal mandate has been the catalyst for state governments across the country to innovate with different tools to strengthen accountability. *Gram panchayat* is the primary program implementing agency of MGNREGA, along with other PRI bodies and line departments. Potential implementation of MGNREGA needs adequate capacitated governing body and motivation.

In this backdrop, this chapter attempts to examine how the institutional features, which are components of good governance, are being practiced through the institutional framework of grassroot level self-government institution. Along with this, attempts had been made to explore the relationship, if any, between the components of good governance and performance of MGNREGA. Thus, *panchayats* have been legally declared as the "principal authorities for planning and implementation" of the Scheme made under the Act. Incidentally, MGNREGA is the first developmental legislation which assigns a definite and important role to PRIs. Further, for realizing entitlements and broadening capabilities of the disadvantaged, democratization and participation are essential and sufficient pre-conditions and only PRIs can bring them about.

9.2 MGNREGA Implementation Mechanism

The implementation of MGNREGA involves institutions at the central government and state level and at all three-tiers of local government in India, which includes the *zila panchayat* at the district level, the *taluk panchayat* at the block level, and the *gram panchayat* at the village level. The most important agency in the central government is the Ministry of Rural Development and the Ministry-founded Central Employment Guarantee Council (CEGC). The Ministry is responsible for ensuring the adequate and timely delivery of resources to the states and for reviewing, monitoring, and evaluating the use of these resources, as well as MGNREGA processes and outcomes. The CEGC advises the central government on MGNREGA-related matters and monitors and evaluates the implementation of the Act. The Council is mandated to prepare annual reports on the implementation of MGNREGA and submit these to the Parliament.

The pivotal institution at the state level is the state government, which is required to formulate a Rural Employment Guarantee Scheme (REGS) that conforms to the minimum features specified under the Act. In addition, the state government must constitute the State Employment Guarantee Council (SEGC), whose main responsibility is to advise the state government on MGNREGA-related matters and to monitor and evaluate the implementation of the Act. Finally, the state government is responsible for ensuring the adequate and timely release of the state's share of the REGS budget and facilitates administrative, financial, and technical support for all implementing bodies at the *zila* (district), *taluk* (block), and *gram* (village) *panchayat* level.

Since MGNREGA foresees a decentralized implementation, the principal authorities for the implementation of the REGS are the local government (panchayat) institutions at the district, block and village level. In order to provide employment in a timely and adequate manner, the local government institutions at all levels must identify priority areas of employment-generating activities and propose, scrutinize, and approve the respective REGS projects.

At the district level, the identification of the REGS projects is guided by the five-year District Perspective Plan, which specifies the long-term employment-generation and development perspectives of the district. In addition to the long-term plan, local government institutions at all levels must also identify the priority activities to be taken up in a year. At the gram panchayat level, these priority areas are decided during village council (gram sabha) and sub-village council (ward sabha) meetings. Based on the recommendations formulated in the *gram sabha* and *ward sabha*, the *gram panchayat* prepares an annual plan and forwards it to the MGNREGA block program officer for technical sanction/approval. Let us now discuss about the role and functions of various implementation agencies.

- **Ministry of Rural Development (MoRD):** The Ministry of Rural Development (MoRD) is the nodal Ministry for the implementation of MGNREGA. It is responsible for setting up of the Central Employment Guarantee Council (CEGC). It has to ensure timely and adequate resource support to the states. It has to undertake regular review, monitoring and evaluation of processes and outcomes. It has to establish a management information system (MIS) to capture and track data on every critical aspect of implementation, and assess the utilization of resources through a set of performance indicators.
- **Central Employment Guarantee Council (CEGC):** The Central Employment Guarantee Council (CEGC) shall be responsible for advising the Central government on MGNREGA-related matters, and for monitoring and evaluating the implementation of the Act. It shall prepare

Annual Reports on the implementation of NREGA and submit these to the Parliament.

- **State Government:** The State Government has to formulate a Rural Employment Guarantee Scheme (REGS), and the rules pertinent to its implementation, in consonance with the Act. It will set up the SEGC (State Employment Guarantee Council), and also designate an officer as the State Rural Employment Guarantee Commissioner responsible for ensuring that all activities required to fulfil the objectives of the Act are carried out. It will ensure that the state's share of the REGS budget is released on time. It will ensure wide communication of the Scheme and dissemination of information regarding its implementation. It will ensure all administrative, financial and technical support to the district programme coordinator, programme officer, PRIs and all other agencies involved in implementation.
- **State Employment Guarantee Council (SEGC):** The State Employment Guarantee Council (SEGC) shall advise the state government on the implementation of the scheme, and evaluate and monitor it. It will also decide on the 'preferred works' to be implemented under REGS, and prepare annual reports for submission to the state legislature.
- **District Panchayat:** The district panchayat will be responsible for finalizing the district plans and for monitoring and supervising the REGS in the district. It can also execute works from among the 50 percent that are not to be executed by the *gram panchayats*.
- **District Programme Co-ordinator (DPC):** The state government will designate a district programme co-ordinator (DPC), who shall be responsible for the overall co-ordination and implementation of the scheme in the district.
- **Intermediate Panchayat (IP):** Intermediate panchayat will be responsible for planning at the block level, and for

monitoring and supervision. It can also be given the responsibility of executing works from among the 50 percent that are not to be executed by the *gram panchayat*.

- **Programme Officer (PO):** A full-time officer will be appointed as the programme officer at the block level, who shall be responsible for coordinating the works undertaken by the *gram panchayat* and the implementing agencies at the block level.
- **Gram Panchayat (GP):** The *gram panchayat* has a pivotal role in the implementation of REGS. It is responsible for planning of works, registering households, issuing job cards, allocating employment, executing 50 percent of the works, and monitoring the implementation of the scheme at the village level.
- **Gram Sabha (GS):** NREGA authorizes the *gram sabha* to recommend works to be taken up under REGS, to monitor and supervise these works, and to conduct social audits of the implementation of the Scheme. In addition, the *gram sabha* should be used extensively for facilitating the implementation of the scheme, by acting as a forum for sharing information about the Scheme, and also in ensuring transparency and accountability.
- **Other Implementing Agencies:** In addition to *panchayats*, line departments, NGOs, central and state government undertakings, and self-help groups (SHGs) can also be identified as implementing agencies.

9.3 Legal Provisions for PRIs under MGNREGA

MGNREGA assigns PRIs, the most critical role in its implementation. Some of the salient provisions illustrating this point are summed up below:

- Section 12(1) mandates the inclusion of representatives of the PRIs in the State Employment Guarantee Council which is the paramount institution at the state level in implementing the Act, with wide ranging powers and functions.

- Section 13 declares the three-tier PRIs as the "principal authorities" for planning and implementation and outlines the functions of intermediate and district level *panchayats* in planning and supervision of implementation. The district programme coordinator, who, in most part of the country, is the district collector, is given an obligation by this section to assist the district panchayat.
- Section 15 speaks of the programme officer at the intermediate panchayat level (and not at the CD block level). It further states that all or any of the functions of the programme officer can be discharged by the *gram panchayat* or any other local authority.
- Section 16 explains the role of the *gram panchayat* and mandates that at least 50 percent of the work in terms of cost has to be implemented through the *gram panchayat*. Further, it has given the responsibility of allocating employment opportunities among the applicants to the *gram panchayat*.
- Section 17 endows the Gram Sabha with the authority to conduct social audit and monitor execution of works.
- Schedule II explains the duties of the *gram panchayat* in registering the household, issue of job cards, assigning of work, maintenance of records etc…Thus, the MGNREG Act assigns a wide ranging role to PRIs right from registering of workers up to monitoring and social audit. It vests powers of planning and implementation (at least 50 percent) with the PRIs and casts an obligation for transparency and accountability on them, especially on the *gram panchayat*. Probably the only deficiency with reference to PRIs is the non-mentioning of the district planning committees (DPCs) in the Act. Ideally, the DPCs should have been assigned the task of coordinating the planning and preparation of the perspective plan, labour budget and the annual plan.

9.4 Governance and Good Governance

Nowadays, the terms 'governance' and 'good governance'

have become the catchwords in the. development discourse. 'Governance' is defined as a process of decision-making and the process by which decisions are implemented. It denotes both political and administrative functions to ensure moral behaviour and ethical conduct in the task of governing (Singh and Singh, 2004). Good governance is, among other things, participatory, transparent and accountable, effective and equitable, and it promotes the rule of law. It ensures that political, social and economic priorities are based on broad consensus in society and that the voices of the poorest and the most vulnerable are heard in decision-making over the allocation of development resources (UNDP, 1997). Absence of good governance acts as a formidable hurdle in the achievement of proper development. It is necessary to provide the best benefit to a large number of people (Bagchi, 2005). UNDP recognizes the following 9 core characteristics of good governance, which are: (i) participation, (ii) rule of law, (iii) transparency, (iv) responsiveness, (v) consensus-oriented, (vi) equity, (vii) effectiveness and efficiency, (viii) accountability, and (ix) strategic vision.

The implication of good governance is manifold as good institutions beget good governance. Institutions matter for both long and short-term because they form the incentive structure of a society and provide the underlying determinants of economic performance. Sharma (2007) rightly pointed out that, many of the items listed on the good governance agenda as pre-conditions for development are actually consequences of it. The implications of good governance are profound as institution building and the promotion of good governance demand simultaneous commitment to economic development. Finally, measuring good governance and overall governmental performance, generally, requires measuring the "outcomes" not just "inputs" (Rotberg, 2004).

Participation, transparency and accountability are the three pillars of good governance. Following the UNDP measures of good governance, we have considered the following components of good governance and comparing them with MGNREGA.

9.4.1 Participation: The MGNREG Act is hailed as a historic landmark that can ensure the democratic privilege of dignified means of livelihood through right to work with participatory processes like social audit and people's plan. The government has referred to it as an *"Act of the people, by the people, and for the people"*. The Act was prepared through a wide range of consultation with people's organizations. The Act addresses itself chiefly to working people and their fundamental right to life with dignity. All men and women should have a voice in decision-making, either directly or through legitimate intermediate institutions that represent their interests. Such broad participation is built on freedom of association and speech, as well as capacities to participate constructively. Towards this end, planning for works at the local level through decentralized and participatory systems becomes necessary. The Act emphasizes that nature of work will be determined in *palli sabha* through participatory people's plans, approved in *gram sabha* and accordingly the shelf of activities would be prepared. The *gram sabha* is further entrusted to take an active role in approval and monitoring of work, and conducting social audit. Meetings of *gram sabha* (meeting of entire village) are necessary.

The Act also empowers ordinary people to play an active role in the implementation of employment guarantee schemes through *gram sabhas* (participatory and representative micro level administrative unit in three-tier panchayat system), social audits, participatory planning and other means. This Act is an important step towards the realization of the right to work. It is also expected to enhance people's livelihoods on a sustained basis, by developing the economic and social infrastructure in rural areas. MGNREGA is the use of the platform for people's participation facilitated by social audit. In this context, it must be remembered that social audit or public audit is a continuous ongoing process, through which people can participate in the monitoring and implementation of the MGNREGA. It was felt that active community participation was particularly important for ensuring transparency and public accountability. Thus, more than any other law, MGNREGA is an Act of the people, by the people and for the people.

9.4.2 Transparency and Accountability: It was believed that decentralization of governance through panchayati raj system will pave the way for more accountable governance where power will be in the hands of the people and they will be capable to wield it against erring elements. But on the contrary, the system was less responsive towards this decentralization of power and village people are still subject to corruption and deficit of effective service delivery.

Transparency and accountability therefore is most crucial to any development paradigm and are two most important requisites for good governance. Transparency is built on the free flow of information. Processes, institutions and information are directly accessible to those concerned with them, and enough information is provided to understand and monitor them. MGNREGA provides for a 100 days of guaranteed employment in one financial year to all rural households, members of which are willing to do manual labour.

The Act not only guarantees wage employment as a right, but also promotes community monitoring through vigilance and monitoring committees, social audit though *gram sabha* and also makes provision for complete transparency as mandated by the Right to Information Act, 2005. Likewise, in order to ensure transparency and reduce corruption, the government is particular that MGNREGA works should be subjected to social auditing by *gram sabha*. Article 17 (1) says that *gram sabha* would monitor all works which are implemented in the *gram panchayat*. Article 17(2) of the MGNREGA says, "the *gram sabha* shall conduct regular social audits of all the projects under the scheme taken up within the *gram panchayat*". Article 17(3) says "the *gram panchayat* shall make available all relevant documents including the muster rolls, bills, vouchers, measurement books, copies of sanction orders and other connected books of account and papers to the *gram sabha* for the purpose of conducting the social audit.

The process of social audit according to the guidelines should include public vigilance and verification of the following 11 stages of implementation of MGNREGA: registration of families, distribution of job cards, receipt of work applications, preparation of shelf of projects and selection of sites, development and approval of technical estimates and issuance of work order, allotment of work to individuals, implementation and supervision of works, payment of unemployment allowance, payment of wages, evaluation of work, mandatory social audit in the *gram sabha* (social audit forum). The guidelines list out various vulnerabilities at each stages and suggests steps to promote transparency and accountability.

Guidelines also delineates in great details how to publicize, collect data and prepare document, procedures to be adopted and mandatory agenda of the Gram Sabha for social audit. Growing realization of need for transparency, accountability and participation has led to creation of space for social audit under MGNREGA. Using this institutional design, many governmental and non-governmental agencies have conducted social audit in last one and half year since the launch of MGNREGA albeit with different approaches and methodologies. It has been observed that mere statutory provisions are not sufficient to promote transparency and accountability in MGNREGA. Demand side needs to be strengthened with awareness about entitlements, capacity building, mobilization and facilitation. Supply side, primarily responsible for follow up actions, should be supported by creating a non-threatening environment and capacity building in record keeping. It is also important to complete the process of devolution to *panchayat* because accountability without power is as absurd as power without accountability.

The Right to Information Act of 2005 ensures and any official information could be obtained by any citizen by mere application and state is liable to furnish the information within 30 days. This Act is another milestone in the history of democracy in India because public access to information instils spirit of accountability and transparency in governance. Right to information is also seen as a corrective instrument to check corruption, overcome unnecessary secrecy and bureaucratic apathy towards citizen's demands. Right to information is a pre-requisite for healthy democratic structure. Indian Parliament enacted the famous Right to Information Act in 2005, which makes access to information as a fundamental right of the people.

Right to Information (RTI) empowers every citizen to seek any information from government offices and access to official documents on request except the information about national security and strategic issues, private matter and matter under judicial consideration. Since the scope of the Act is broad, RTI has revolutionized the concept of democratic governance substantially. Hence, when MGNREGA was enacted by Indian Parliament in August 2005, RTI was made as an integral part of the Act. It is envisaged that MGNREGA will be meaningless without proper use of RTI because RTI can check corruption and leakage of public funding on MGNREGA in an effective manner. Above all, the provisions of RTI make the implementing agency more transparent and accountable to common masses.

9.4.3 Effectiveness and Efficiency: The efficiency and effectiveness of any program is that processes and institutions produce results that meet needs while making the best use of resources. As far as MGNREGA was concerned, there were two challenges before the effective implementation of MGNREGA. The first was the capacity of the Indian state to meet the huge financial obligations that the law brings in. The other was that even if this law was passed and money made available, corruption would ensure that much of the money would go into the pockets of middlemen. The issue that the implementation mechanism for this programme envisages planning and execution at local level, provides ample opportunities for middle men to siphon out the money, depriving the deserved ones. Critics feel that it would be difficult to ensure the implementation of this guarantee in a vast country like India without compromising on the provisions of transparency and accountability. This has still remained a great concern in implementation of this Act throughout the country even after nine years.

The overall fund utilisation in the MGNREGA has plummeted to 60 percent. Most states are unable to utilise even half of the funds slotted for administrative expenses, stalling administrative reforms that are expected to increase the efficiency of the scheme. Administrative costs are important because the money is used to improve the knowledge base of the scheme like technology, monitoring mechanisms, infrastructure, personnel capacity etc. The states can use 6 percent of allocation under the scheme for administrative purposes—to build capacity for the kind of expenditure the scheme targets to ensure income support for the poor. The overall utilisation of funds for administrative costs under the scheme was 40.3 percent in 2010-11.

The second challenge needs to be seriously addressed by all quarters. Corruption is a serious problem that could undermine all the objectives of this significant, radical, and hard won entitlement for India's rural poor. The question of leakages need to be addressed not just to answer the critics, but also to ensure that the benefits of this legislation reach to those it was supposed to. The ghost of corruption has haunted many public interventions in India, and the MGNREGA is no exception. Bank payments of MGNREGA wages were recently introduced on a mass scale, and projected as a foolproof remedy against corruption. Recent evidence, however, suggests that the banking system itself is not above corruption—corrective steps are urgently needed. The effectiveness of MGNREGA also crucially depends on what type of schemes it gives priority to. Lack of focus of social, gender inequality in creation of productive assets has been a major reason for limited success of wage employment programme.

9.4.4 Equity: Equality of men and women in decision-making to improve or maintain their well-being—one major provision of MGNREGA is employment generation without gender discrimination. Through this, it will provide and protect the justice and rights of women. There is much that the MGNREGA promises from the perspective of women's empowerment as well. Most boldly, in a rural milieu marked by stark inequalities between men and women—in the opportunities for gainful employment afforded as well as wage rates—MGNREGA represents action on both these counts. The Act stipulates that wages will be equal for men and women. It is also committed to ensuring that at least 33 percent of the workers shall be women. By generating employment for women at fair wages in the village, MGNREGA can play a substantial role in economically empowering women and laying the basis for greater independence and self-esteem. It would be worthwhile to recognize the significant achievements of MGNREGA with regard to: (a) gender parity of wages, (b) mobilization of women for MGNREGA employment, and (c) increase in rights of women over earnings from the MGNREGA.

In contrast to the high participation of women in the programme as workers, their participation in processes like work selection, social audit, mobilization of civil society, and share in the control and management of assets created is not encouraging. This being the case, in some places, women's participation in the *gram sabha* has still increased, and there is even an increase in the number of women who speak in the *gram sabhas*. There are also some examples of women groups playing an important role in the management of community assets.

Technological change and economic development policies need to be supported by programmes for equality-based gender institutions at micro and macro-levels. Self-help groups (SHGs), *mahila mandals* (rural women's organizations), gender responsive *panchayat*, community-based organizations (such as SEWA, Working Women's Forum, Kudumbashree, and numerous rural NGOs working on MGNREGA implementation) can be efficient models of such institutional arrangement at the local level.

These organizations can play an active role in widening the outreach of both technological information and spreading awareness on women's control rights over productive assets and incomes earned through the guaranteed employment and otherwise. Such an approach will enable poor rural women and men to have greater access to institutional credit, promote greater bargaining power against unjust social and economic practices and facilitate implementation of MGNREGA programmes. However, capacity building improvement of members of SHGs through skill training and mandatory measure of gender equality in management and control rights to productive assets are critical, only then it would be possible for SHGs to act as an effective agency for rural development under MGNREGA.

Importantly, a majority of the women workers under MGNREGA programme say that such employment has brought a significant change in their communities and in their own lives; the MGNREGA wages are higher than the market wages and it has improved their spending capacity. Women are able to use their earnings for household food and consumption needs, healthcare and education of children. More importantly, earlier they used to be dependent on their husbands for any expenses, but now with some cash in their hands, women have greater degree of economic independence and self- confidence and they feel empowered, as they are now also the earning members of the family. Equal rights to productive assets of women with those of men, can lead to greater economic activity, change in the perception of dependence on men, and thus would result in substantially reducing the exclusion of women from social processes and promote development of diverse capabilities, thereby enhancing the productivity and reducing inequalities.

This narrative about responding to people's protest about poverty through introduction of a right-based approach for poverty alleviation in the form of provision of rural employment guarantee in the constitutional system of India suggests that the MGNREGA has inaugurated a remarkable process for the empowerment of the poor. The Act is particularly a tool of empowerment for the most vulnerable sections of the village communities as they are also victims of social exclusion and political marginalization. Moreover, it has stimulated mobilization of the poor for livelihood within the legitimate framework of governance. Also, MGNREGA has made a dent on poverty by both increasing employment opportunities and raising the wage rate. Perhaps, it has strengthened the process of participatory democracy through economic decentralization and by giving significant roles to the panchayati raj institutions (PRIs), the rural poor classes, and the civil society groups.

References

Aiyar, Y. and S. Samji (2009), "Guaranteeing Good Governance: Understanding the Effectiveness of Accountability Mechanism in NREGA", NREGA e-Knowledge Network; *UNDP,* New Delhi.

Bagchi, K.K. (2005), "Good Governance and Sustainable Local Development: A Case Study of GPs in West Bengal".

Comptroller and Auditor General (2008), "Performance Audit of Implementation of National Rural Employment Guarantee Act, 2005 (NREGA)", Performance Audit Report No. 42, New Delhi, Comptroller and Auditor General of India.

Drèze, J. and C. Oldiges (2007), "Commendable Act", *Frontline,* 24 (14).

Drèze, J. and R. Khera (2008), "From Accounts to Accountability", *The Hindu,* December 6.

Drèze, J., R. Khera, and Siddhartha (2007), "NREGA in Orissa: Ten Loopholes and the Silver Lining", Interim Survey Report, October 21, Allahabad, University of Allahabad, http://www.righttofoodindia.org/data/gbpant07orissa-social-audit-interim-report.pdf, Accessed March 21, 2009.

Government of India (2005), "Operational Guidelines: the National Rural Employment Guarantee Act, 2005 (NREGA)", Ministry of Rural Development, Department of Rural Development, New Delhi.

Islam, Nazrul Md. (2004), "Decentralized Governance Transparency and Accountability: Empirical Evidence from West Bengal", ISEC Working Paper 144, Institute for Social and Economic Change.

Jhilam, Roychowdhury (2010), "Right To Information and National Rural Employment Guarantee Acts: An Attempt towards More Accountable and Transparent Governance", *Global Media Journal,* December.

Maitreesh, Ghatak and Maitreya Ghatak (2002), "Recent Reforms in the Panchayat System in West Bengal: Towards Greater Participatory Governance"?, *Economic and Political Weekly*, Vol. 37, No. 1, January 5-11.

North, Douglass C. (2005), "Understanding the Process of Economic Change", Princeton, NJ: Princeton University Press.

Rao, V.M. (2007), "Making Safety Nets Effective for Hardcore Poor", *Economic and Political Weekly*, August 18.

Robert Rotberg (2004), "Strengthening Governance", *Washington Quarterly,* 28, No. 1, pp. 71-81.

Shah, Amita and Sunny Jose, (2008), "Asset Creation and Local Economy under NREGS: Scope and Challenges", Paper presented at International Seminar on National Rural Employment Guarantee Scheme in India, September 16-17, New Delhi.

Sharma, Shailendra D. (2007), "Democracy, Good Governance, and Economic Development", *Taiwan Journal of Democracy*, Vol. 3, No. 1, pp. 29-62.

Singh and Singh (2004), "Governance and Development Deprivation in India", *The Indian Journal of Public Administration,* Vol. L, No. 1, January-March, pp. 277-284.

UNDP (1997), "Governance for Sustainable Human Development", A UNDP Policy Paper, UNDP.

Vijayakumar, B. and Sajan N. Thomas (2008), "Governance, Institutions, and National Rural Employment Guarantee Scheme: A Study on Peermadi Panchayat in Kerala", Paper presented at International Seminar on National Rural Employment Guarantee Scheme in India, September 16-17, New Delhi.

10

MGNREGA and Technological Innovations

10.1 UID and MGNREGA

The Unique Identification (UID) project, a flagship project, managed by the Unique Identification Authority of India (UIDAI) is an ambitious plan of issuing a unique biometric-enabled number, innocuously called "Aadhaar", to every Indian resident. It has also begun to generate a debate on citizen-state relations, privacy, financial implications, and operational practicalities. What the debate has largely missed so far, however, is the credibility of the UIDAI's claims in the field of social policy, particularly the Mahatma Gandhi National Rural Employment Guarantee Act (MGNREGA) and Public Distribution System (PDS).

A number of benefit claims which the project possesses—the power to eliminate financial exclusion, enhance accessibility, and uplift living standards for the majority poor etc.—have been underlined by the UIDAI. The UID is projected as an innovative and revolutionary initiative, with unprecedented gains in efficiency and transparency. The ability of UID to positively establish and authenticate the identity of every individual can overcome many of the challenges faced by targeted benefit programmes. Here, we will discuss the various opportunities and challenges offered by UID for implementation of the MGNREGA.

10.2 UID Powered MGNREGA

Incorporation of UID into the MGNREGA programme will assist in addressing some of the major challenges faced by this Scheme that impedes its progress and performance. The major aspects that can be addressed and ways of addressing them are as follows.

10.2.1 Payment of Wages: Payment of wages remains one of the major challenges faced by MGNREGA due to corruption, delay of payments and other leakages. Wherever possible, these payments are supposed to be automated through local bank branches or through post offices. In many areas, the wages continue to be paid in the form of cash. The UID can fully replace the need to provide supporting documentation for the standard, know your customer (KYC) fields, making opening a bank account significantly simpler. Arrangements of seamlessly opening a bank account in the name of one of the family members at the time of job card issue with embedded UID can also be explored.

10.2.2 Theft from Beneficiaries: One form of corruption in MGNREGA is 'theft from beneficiaries' where officials under-pay workers for the work they have done. The responsibility of determining and authenticating the amount of work done under MGNREGA lies in the hands of official supervisors who are prone to siphoning-off the funds. The system of UID authentication when introduced at the site of work can ensure that there is a match between the hours of work claimed by the worker and the official supervising the site. The ability of UID to identify the presence of a specific individual also makes it much easier to centrally monitor delinquency among government servants who are authenticating the work and checking whether the allocated work was completed satisfactorily.

10.2.3 Theft from Taxpayers: The study also threw light on another form of corruption which the researchers called 'theft from taxpayers' wherein the officials over-reported the amount of work done when they sent their reports up the hierarchy. This effort can be corroborated against the wages paid to beneficiaries establishing the execution of the project. Suspicious activity can be flagged and verified by an appropriate government official.

10.2.4 Ghost Beneficiaries: Once each citizen in a job card needs to provide his UID before claiming employment, the potential for ghost or fictitious beneficiaries is eliminated. A further reinforcement of paying only to real citizens will happen by way of opening bank accounts with UIDs.

Table: 10.1: Aadhaar Enabled MGNREGA

Current Issues	How Aadhaar can Address Challenges?
Duplicate/fake beneficiary lists	Aadhaar biometric de-duplication will ensure unique genuine beneficiaries
Exclusion of residents without proper identification documents	Aadhaar could provide identity and address proof to seek job cards
Difficulties in demanding work	Work can be demanded by using Aadhaar authentication through mobile or kiosk enabling timely employment or unemployment wages
Attendance at work sites	Aadhaar authentication could guarantee worker presence at work site and improve accountability of the work supervisor
Lack of choice and mobility	Aadhaar authentication is not restricted to any one area; providing choice and mobility to the residents
Payments	Aadhaar enabled micro payments platform could help in efficient payment of wages through micro ATMs/BCs
Grievance handling and fraud analytics	Aadhaar could enable fast grievance reporting and resolution through mobile or online channels

10.2.5 Beneficiary Misuse: UID will ensure that misuse by claiming benefits under multiple job cards is avoided. The UID de-duplication process which will assure a positive identification of every resident in the country, can overcome the challenge of uniquely identifying every worker.

10.2.6 Beneficiary Management: The UID system will provide an excellent platform for managing citizens who relocate or migrate from one place to another and want to seamlessly enjoy benefits of the programme.

10.2.7 Social Audit: The village level social audit committee can be selected after authentication with the UID database. The social audit reports filed by the village level committees can be authenticated by the biometrics of the committee members and the social audit coordinator.

10.2.8 Transparency: The above benefits combined with the positive beneficiary identification will ensure that accurate details of benefits can be published providing greater transparency at the individual beneficiary level.

10.3 MGNREGA Reforms for UID

To effectively leverage the UID program, the MGNREGA scheme will need to be modified to incorporate the UID number into beneficiary interactions. In order to accommodate UID authentication, MGNREGA will need to reengineer its business processes.

The most basic requirement for change will be in the form of incorporating the UID method of authentication.

Work sites will have to adhere to norms and procedures specified by the UIDAI for fingerprint capture and verification, and introduce a robust biometric authentication process at every point.

The key areas in the MGNREGA process that need to be addressed are summarized below.

10.3.1 UID in Job Cards: The job cards will need to be updated with the UID numbers of all family members. This could be accomplished by issuing a new job card or by collecting and incorporating the UID numbers into the beneficiary database without reissue of the job cards.

10.3.2 UID in Muster Rolls: The muster rolls should contain a reference to the UID of the citizen who is earning wages. This should be incorporated at the time of allocation of the labour to the project (works).

10.3.3 UID in Bank Account: The UID should be incorporated with the bank/post office account information of a beneficiary to which the wages are being paid. Mechanism to encourage bank/post office to incorporate the UID into their systems is being pursued.

10.3.4 Transaction Authentication: The transaction authentication against the UID database should be implemented at different citizen touch points starting with the job card. The ideal situation would be the recording of attendance on a handheld system using biometric authentication. UID will also endeavour to introduce a biometric authentication for amount withdrawal from the account into which wages are being paid.

The above change can be implemented in the MGNREGA programme with minimal effort. There are also synergies with other government programmes such as TPDS that can be explored which can further ease the implementation in such areas like handheld deployment.

10.4 Issues Related with UID Implementation

The UIDAI has a four-page document on MGNREGA. From this document, it is clear that its officials are poorly informed on issues relating to MGNREGA. Resulting from its poor understanding of the programme are several claims of improving efficiency in government spending like controlling corruption in MGNREGA, eliminating financial exclusion, preventing exclusion from government programmes due to the lack of identity proof, and so on. One good example of the UIDAI being poorly informed is its statement regarding MGNREGA wage payments. The UIDAI claims that the UID will enable financial inclusion, but it seems to be unaware that wage payments through banks and post offices became mandatory in 2008. The transition to bank payments is now largely complete. A large majority of MGNREGA workers already have a bank (or post office) account—10.02 crore accounts of MGNREGA workers have been opened and about 90 percent of wages have been disbursed through these accounts up to March 2014. This is not to say that the opening of bank accounts was a smooth process.

The main hurdle is not about the know your customer (KYC) norms (as claimed by the UIDAI) but that the coverage of banks and post offices in rural areas is inadequate, the ones that exist are under-staffed, and post offices in many parts do not maintain computerized records. Tamil Nadu is the only state that still makes cash payments, on the grounds that it is able to control leakages within the cash system and that cash payments help to ensure timely disbursal of wages. Field evidence suggests that there is some truth in this claim of the Tamil Nadu government (Khera and Muthiah, 2010). The claim of controlling corruption through the UID is made on the premise that payments are still being made in cash. In the case of cash payments of MGNREGA wages, the main source of embezzlement used to be by fudging attendance records—by either adding names of people who had not worked, or inflating the attendance of those who had worked. Payment of wages through banks and post offices has made wage corruption quite difficult.

However, three potential channels for siphoning off money remain open—extortion, collusion and deception. Extortion means that when "inflated" wages are withdrawn by the labourer, the middleman turns extortionist and takes his share from him or her. Collusion means that the labourer and the middlemen agree to share the inflated wages that are credited to the labourer's account. Deception means that middlemen open and operate accounts on behalf of labourers, withdraw the inflated wages from these bank accounts, pay workers their due in cash, and pocket the difference. Biometric-enabled UID to authenticate identity can help to prevent "deception", but is of little use in preventing collusion or extortion.

The UIDAI has set itself a target of covering only half of India's population in the next few years. The UIDAI is engaging man registrars to meet its targets. In its eagerness to de-duplicate, there is a danger that the UID will be made compulsory in a rushed manner. Even with an ambitious target, the project will then end up *excluding* large sections of India's population. Hasty integration of UID with the PDS or MGNREGA could, in practice, go against the rhetoric on "inclusivity".

In fact, a "reengineering" of the MGNREGA is currently

underway. This involves the engagement of "service providers" who will be responsible for enrolling individuals for UID, and at a later stage, involved in authentication (including at the worksite using hand-held devices) of workers. The consequences of this sort of re-engineering are likely to be disastrous for the MGNREGA. If, for example, the Ministry of Rural Development links the provision of new job cards to getting a UID, many workers are likely to be denied work for sometime to come.

There is a real danger that those who do not enrol will be turned away from the MGNREGA. We have already learnt this lesson—the hard way—when the transition to bank payments was made. Poorly equipped and understaffed banks and post offices were expected to open millions of MGNREGA accounts overnight. Those workers who did not have accounts were denied work.

Facilitating "doorstep banking" through banking correspondent (BC model) is supposed to be another benefit of the UID. At the moment, labourers often have to go long distances to withdraw their wages. Banking correspondents (intermediaries who extend banking services to remote villages) are supposed to enable disbursal of wages at their doorstep. Here again, however, there are issues of practicality and effectiveness, and we need to consider alternatives. Modernizing and computerizing post offices would also contribute to making banking services accessible.

As a long-term measure, the government should consider an expansion of the rural banking network. Appointment of local *kirana* stores as banking correspondents could be a regressive step, as it would mean routing MGNREGA wages through the local *bania* (often a moneylender also). The BC model could end up diluting the sanctity of existing banking practices. At the end of the day, it is not clear from the UIDAI documents exactly how UID is supposed to help MGNREGA.

There is no obvious problem of "identity fraud" in MGNREGA that UID is waiting to resolve. There is no evidence, for instance, of fake job cards being a major problem. An MGNREGA job card is not like a PDS ration card, which automatically entitles the holder to subsidized grain. To get benefits under the MGNREGA, the job cardholder is required to work—so a fake job card is of little use *per se*. Claiming benefits without working requires collusion between non-working job cardholders and implementing officials. If the two parties collude, some job cardholders can have wages credited to their bank accounts, by getting on muster rolls. UID purports to prevent this through "biometric attendance at the worksite", but the practicality of this imaginative idea is far from clear—it could easily create more problems than it resolves. And some form of collusion can persist even with biometric attendance at the worksite. For the MGNREGA, the UID, if it works, will help to plug some minor loopholes. This does not justify the sweeping claims that are being made.

There are significant synergies between the MGNREGA and the UID programme allowing improved implementation of the MGNREGA programme with an increased transparency and its accountability. The UID programme benefits by increased enrolment and an opportunity to capture changes to beneficiary data.

11

Kerala Model of MGNREGA

MGNREGA has been hailed as a revolutionary scheme and it has been maintained that it would have an impact on poverty in a major way by building infrastructure and enhancing growth in rural areas. Kannan (2005) has stressed that the potential of NREGA could be more fully realized if human development had been more fully prioritized, including, for instance, improved childcare facilities, which would help mothers to work under the scheme. Thus, MGNREGA would lead to empowerment of various sections of society, that is 'the development of personal competencies and skills, to the process of challenging the existing power relations, household decision-making, gaining access, control over resources like credit, income, land, knowledge, and subjective variables like sense of personal power and self-efficacy'.

The choice of works suggested in the Act addresses causes of chronic poverty like drought, deforestation and soil erosion, so that the process of employment generation is maintained on a sustainable basis. A well-designed employment guarantee programme can, under favourable circumstances, promote job creation, gender equality and pro-poor development. MGNREGA has great potential for increasing the volume of employment among the rural unemployed and underemployed. It provides ample opportunities for creating rural public assets, which has been largely neglected. It will help to enhance the purchasing power of rural households, thereby contributing to poverty alleviation. It also has the capacity to tap the hitherto under-utilized labour of women in developing rural India. By providing equal wages to both men and women, MGNREGA upholds the social position and integrity of women and thus promotes gender equality (Rania Antonopoulos, 2009).

This chapter focuses on a specific study based on the secondary data. The relevant data has been collected from the website of Ministry of Rural Development, Government of India and has been used for various analytical purposes like employment generation, especially among SCs, STs, and women in the state of Kerala. The unemployment data has been collected from employment directorate of Kerala. In this chapter, attempts have been made to analyse the effectiveness of MGNREGA in employment generation, especially in the state of Kerala.

11.1 Problem of Unemployment in Kerala

Today, the problem of unemployment is the single largest puzzle and has been a burning issue in the Kerala economy. Kerala has the highest unemployment rate among the states of India which accounts for about 25.5 percent. Unemployment is said to prevail when supply of labour exceeds its demand. That is, unemployment exists, if all able bodied men are not able to work at the existing wage rate. Growth of supply of labour is determined by population growth and participation of population in the total work force. In Kerala, from the decade of 1970s onwards, there has been a rapid rise in the labour supply because of the increase in the number of women seeking wage employment. Thus, though the supply of work seekers increased, the demand for them did not increase. As a consequence, there was an alarming increase in unemployment rate from time to time.

The labour force participation in Kerala is one of the lowest (31 percent) in the country. If we take into consideration all workers (main and marginal) into account, the female work participation rate in Kerala declined from 16.61 percent in 1981 to 15.85 percent in 1991. On the contrary, the male work participation rate increased from 44.89 percent to 47.58 percent during the period 1981-1991. The growth rate of employment is also extremely slow. In fact, an important dimension of Kerala's economic crisis is the acute and ever-rising level of unemployment.

For instance, while Kerala accounts for only 4 percent of

India's population, its share in India's unemployed is as high as 16 percent. Work seekers registered in the employment exchange increased from 0.7 million in 1975 to nearly 3 million in 1990, the later represents close to 30 percent of the work force. There may be some over estimation in this source since some of those who were registered may be engaged in some gainful employment off late (Mukherjee and Isaac, 1991).

Looking at the political economy of labour and development in Kerala, Kannan (1998) argues that there is a mismatch between labour supply and labour demand, as a result of changing job expectations of the younger generations in a technologically stagnant economy. Moreover, the rural labour market in Kerala exhibits a paradox of high unemployment and high wages (Nair, 1997). Although, the Government introduced the Employment Guaranteed Scheme in 2006, in spite of creation of some unskilled manual work, the scheme was not able to remove the problem of unemployment, because the problem of unemployment is not like the one in Kerala, where there exists a huge educational unemployment.

The unemployment problem in Kerala is not only about educational unemployment but also simple unemployment of semi-skilled and unskilled workers. This is the highest in the country and is on the rise, too. One important feature of Kerala's economy, which makes it different from the rest of the country is the net out-migration of labour force, particularly to Gulf region and inflow of huge remittances into the state. Huge out-migration, as has been rightly pointed out, happens mainly because of lack of employment opportunities. The worsening unemployment situation is obviously related to the inability of the economy of the state to generate any fresh employment during the last few years (Table 11.1).

While this phenomenon of "jobless growth" is observable in all the states of the country, the situation in Kerala appears to be particularly distressing since most of the labour intensive/labour absorbing traditional industries depending on exports, are facing a survival crisis in the liberalized trade environment.

Table 11.1: Employment and Unemployment Indicators in Kerala in 2004-05 and 2009-10

Indica-tors	Rural			Urban		
	Males	Females	Males+ Females	Males	Females	Males+ Females
NSS 61st Round (July 2004-June 2005)						
Usual Principal Status						
LFPR	572	258	407	565	260	410
WPR	524	178	343	514	149	329
UR	83	309	158	90	429	199
Usual Status (ps+ss)						
LFPR	589	321	448	583	301	440
WPR	559	256	400	547	200	371
UR	51	201	107	62	334	154
Current Weekly Status						
LFPR	568	285	420	560	260	408
WPR	512	211	354	510	165	335
UR	98	260	156	91	365	180
Current Daily Status						
LFPR	548	246	390	544	240	390
WPR	432	161	290	450	139	292
UR	211	346	256	174	423	252
NSS 66th Round (July 2009-June 2010)						
Usual Principal Status						
LFPR	572	223	389	553	213	375
WPR	550	176	354	534	171	344
UR	38	210	90	34	198	83
Usual Status (ps+ss)						
LFPR	583	260	414	564	233	391
WPR	564	218	383	547	194	363
UR	32	161	75	29	168	73
Current Weekly Status						
LFPR	566	238	394	555	218	379
WPR	539	191	357	526	179	344
UR	47	199	95	52	181	91
Current Daily Status						
LFPR	541	213	370	534	201	360
WPR	471	155	306	469	158	307
UR	129	274	173	121	213	148

Source: NSSO Reports on Employment and Unemployment Situation in India.

Unemployment and under employment among workers in the traditional sectors is indeed a cause for concern. One of the most important groups of such workers is the traditional agricultural workers. According to the 2001 Census, the number of agricultural workers in Kerala were around 16.20 lakh and this is more than twice the number of cultivators (7.20 lakh) and more than four times the number in the household industry (3.70 lakh). Close to three-fourths of workers in the household industry are in rural areas and nearly half of them are female workers. Both rural and urban female unemployment rate has increased dramatically. According to the National Sample Survey, unemployment rate (unemployed as a percent of the labour force) was 21 percent in Kerala in 1999-2000.

National Sample Survey Organization (NSSO) has been conducting household surveys on the subject of employment-unemployment in India at periodic intervals with the aim of getting estimates on level of parameters of various employment and unemployment characteristics at national and state level. The results of the Survey, conducted for the period July 2009-June 2010 (as part of 66th Round of NSSO survey programme) were released in July 2011. Estimates on indicators of employment and unemployment are obtained by the NSSO in three different approaches used for classification of the activity status of the person. These are as follows.

- Number of persons usually unemployed based on usual status approach—which itself worked out in two different methods—one, the principal status (PS) method, which indicates the numerical magnitude of the persons unemployed for a relatively longer period during a reference period of 365 days and the other, the usual status (adjusted) or usual status (ps+ss) method—here the number of unemployed is arrived at by excluding those employed in a subsidiary capacity during the reference period. The number arrived in second method will be lower than the former as some persons categorized as unemployed according to the first method might be working in a subsidiary capacity and these persons are excluded in the second method.

- Number of persons unemployed on an average in a week, based on the current weekly status (CWS) approach.
- Number of persons-days unemployed on an average, on a day during the reference period of seven days preceding the date of survey, based on the current daily status (CDS) approach.

The 2009-10 survey reveals that among the Indian states, Kerala had the highest unemployment rate (16.7 percent) based on current daily status approach; followed by Nagaland (15 percent). In Kerala, unemployment rate among males was 12.7 percent and that among females was 25.9 percent, based on the CDS approach. In rural areas, the unemployment rate was estimated at 17.3 percent (males: 12.9 percent and females: 27.4 percent), whereas in urban areas, it was estimated at 14.8 percent (males: 12.1 percent and females: 21.3 percent). As per the survey conducted in 2009-10, the unemployment rate (UR) in India was estimated at 6.6 percent under the current daily status (CDS) approach as against 8.2 percent based on the 2004-05 survey. Unemployment rate was found to be higher in rural areas than in urban areas; it was 6.8 percent in rural areas compared to 5.8 percent in urban areas. Unemployment rate among rural females was 8 percent compared to 6.4 percent for rural males; urban female unemployment rate was 9.1 percent compared to 5.1 percent for urban males. In rural areas, the unemployment rate among males was 8.0 percent as per the 2004-05 sample survey.

This rate diminished to 6.4 percent as per the 2009-10 sample survey. In the urban areas, the unemployment rate among males decreased from 7.5 percent to 5.1 percent during the five-year period. Among rural females, the unemployment rate decreased from 8.7 percent to 8.0 percent and among urban females, from 11.6 percent to 9.1 percent during the same period.

In 2011, 1.05 million of Kerala's population was

unemployed, i.e. 4,65,000 males and 5,80,000 females. The corresponding numbers in 2008 were 3,80,000 males 3,98,000 females taking the total unemployed to 7,79,000 persons. The unemployment rate (as percent of labour force) was 10.5 percent in 2011 [6.4 among males and 22.3 among females] (Table 11.2). The unemployment rate in 2008 was 8.6 percent [5.6 percent among males and 17.8 percent among females]. Thus, the period 2008-2011 saw a fairly large increase (more than a quarter of a million) in unemployment in Kerala.

Table 11.2: Number and Rate of Unemployment by District, 2011

Districts	Number of Unemployed			Unemployment Rate (in percent)		
	Males	Females	Total	Males	Females	Total
Thiruvanantha-puram	64660	43937	108597	9.0	18.4	11.4
Kollam	38157	47087	85244	6.6	22.4	10.9
Pathanamthitta	26453	15410	41863	8.5	46.1	12.2
Alappuzha	29809	85680	115489	6.5	30.3	15.6
Kottayam	33508	79160	112668	7.0	25.2	14.2
Idukki	15933	14980	30913	5.8	14.9	8.3
Ernakulum	39532	60014	99545	4.7	24.7	9.3
Thrissur	52015	24014	76029	8.6	14.9	9.9
Palakkad	35435	37384	72819	5.3	15.1	7.9
Malappuram	35300	19556	54857	4.7	16.4	6.3
Kozhikode	25450	32345	57795	3.8	19.9	6.9
Wayanad	8029	7545	15574	4.0	10.7	5.7
Kannur	32337	79721	112059	6.7	36.8	16.1
Kasaragod	28825	32986	61811	8.5	22.0	12.6
Kerala	465444	579819	1045262	6.4	22.3	10.5

Source*:* Directorate of Employment, Kerala, 2011.

Unemployment is relatively high at the South-end and North-end of the state. The highest rate, 16.1 was in Kannur district. The lowest rate was in Wayanad district at just 5.7 percent. The southern districts, Thiruvananthapuram to Kottayam had relatively high unemployment rates. Kozhikode and Wayanad districts had relatively low male unemployment rates. Thiruvananthapuram district in the extreme south and Kasaragod district in extreme north had the highest rates at 9.0 percent and 8.5 percent respectively.

Unemployment arises due to several factors such as low rate of economic growth, changing profile of the work force, lack of appropriate educational system and lack of opportunities. In Kerala, these factors have substantially contributed to large scale unemployment. As the economy developed, the demand for unskilled and less skilled labour seems to have declined. On the other hand, the demand for skilled labour—on account of technological development and up gradation and changes in the organization of work—has begun to increase. The demand for multi skilled workers has also started rising.

At the same time, the overall rate of growth in employment got accelerated by more than the rate of deceleration of workforce. The organized sector is not growing enough to absorb work seekers. Significant employment generation is taking place in tertiary/service sector activities. The unorganized/informal sector employment is also increasing due to various reasons. One such reason is the entrepreneur's strategy to remain small or tiny to avoid labour laws.

The Employment Department and the Industrial Training Department play a complementary role in providing employment to the unemployed registered labour force in the state. The former undertakes skill training to make the manpower marketable and the latter looks after the needs of the work seekers. All categories of employment seekers above the age of 14 are allowed to register at the employment exchanges. According to the Employment Directorate, 43.28 lakh employment seekers were there in the live register of employment exchanges as on 30.06.2010 of which, 25.47 lakh were females. In Kerala, the total number of work seekers in 2007 was 39.88 lakh. The number of job seekers increased to

41.44 lakh in 2008, to 43 lakh in 2009 and upto 43.43 lakh in June 2011. The percentage of work seekers below SSLC to the total work seekers showed a decreasing trend and the percentage of work seekers who possess SSLC and above showed an increasing trend. The trend of work seekers in Kerala since 2001 is shown below in Table 11.3.

Table: 11.3: Number of Work Seekers in Kerala during 2001-2011 (in lakh)

Year	Below SSLC		SSLC and Above		Total Work Seekers (in lakh)
	Persons	Percent	Persons	Percent	
2001	9.67	21.8	34.64	78.2	44.31
2002	7.12	19.3	29.68	80.7	36.80
2003	7.46	18.6	32.58	81.4	40.05
2004	6.73	17.9	30.83	82.1	37.56
2005	6.29	17.1	30.41	82.9	36.70
2006	6.37	16.5	32.19	83.5	38.57
2007	6.31	15.8	33.58	84.2	39.89
2008	6.22	15.1	35.22	85.00	41.44
2009	6.24	14.50	36.76	85.49	43.00
2010	5.94	13.87	37.27	86.12	43.28
2011	5.86	13.50	37.56	86.50	43.43

Source: Directorate of Employment, Kerala, 2011.

The number of work seekers below SSLC has been on a declining trend. They declined from 9.67 lakh in 2001 to 6.29 lakh in 2005. They further declined to 5.94 lakh in 2010 and again declined to 5.86 lakh in August 2011. The total number of work seekers who possess SSLC and above increased from 30.41 lakh in 2005 to 37.27 lakh in 2010, and further increased to 37.56 lakh in August 2011. The percentage of work seekers who possess below SSLC to the total work seekers has shown a decreasing trend. Whereas the percentage of work seekers who possess SSLC and its above have shown an increasing trend.

Government of Kerala introduced an unemployment assistance scheme in 1982 for the unemployed through the Department of National Employment Service. As per the Kerala Panchayati Raj and Municipalities Act, 1994, the scheme of unemployment assistance was transferred to the local bodies and the powers for inviting applications for unemployment allowances, processing of applications after the scrutiny of employment officers, sanctioning and the distribution of unemployment allowances were vested with the local bodies. The amount of unemployment allowances provided in the budget is allotted to the Employment Department and the department distributes the amount to local bodies as per their requirements.

The annual family income of the applicant should not be above ₹ 12,000 (per annum) and personal income should not be above ₹ 100 per month. The candidates should have passed SSLC and should possess three years registration seniority after attaining 18 years of age. The candidates belonging to SCs/STs and PH should have appeared in the SSLC examination through proper schools. The physically handicapped (PH) candidates need a registration seniority of two years after attaining 18 years of age. The upper age limit is 35 years. Students are not eligible for applying for unemployment allowances scheme. There are 3,37,032 beneficiaries in the state under the scheme.

11.2 Migration in Kerala

Growing unemployment has led to increased out-migration of workers to other states within the country and abroad, to the Gulf countries in particular. The phenomenon of migration, especially to the Gulf countries, has had a positive effect on economic growth—at least raising the consumption level—due to increasing migrants' remittances, which is estimated to be equal to about one-third of the gross state domestic product. Interestingly, while Kerala is not among the high per capita income states, its ranks first among the top states in terms of per capita consumption. That is why, Kerala is known as a "consumer state". The increasing flow of migrants' remittance has an obvious impact on raising the demand for quality of public services.

A society that heavily depends on out-migration as a solution to growing unemployment and the migrant's remittances as a source for improved standards of living makes heavy demand for education services, especially on quality education to compete in the international market for employment.

Remittances represent an important lifeline for a large number of people and constitute an enormous transfer of private sources from migrants to their families in labour sending communities. The importance of remittances in the Kerala economy is well documented.

Remittance from emigrants abroad to Kerala in 2011 were estimated to be approximately ₹ 49,695 crore compared to ₹ 43,288 crore in 2008. Remittances were ₹ 63,315 per household in 2011 compared to ₹ 57,227 in 2008. Increase in remittances during 2008-2011 (15 percent) was much larger than the increase in the number of emigrants (4 percent).

The migratory flow has diminished the access to health care and services for individuals who depend on public health care system in the state. The migration study conducted by Centre for Development Studies (CDS) in 2002 attempted to conduct a time series estimation of remittances from abroad to the Kerala economy for the period 1972 to 2000. Reliable estimates of the quantum of such remittances over time have been difficult to obtain. The study finds that by the early 1990s remittance to the Kerala economy assumed a significant share in state's income. It ranged from 17 percent during 1991-92 to 24 percent during 1997-98 with an average of 22 percent in the second half of the 1990s. It was estimated that in 1998, there were 13.62 lakh Kerala migrants abroad. The 2011 CDS survey had estimated the number of Kerala migrants abroad at 2.28 million, up from 2.19 million in 2008, 1.84 million in 2003 and 1.36 million in 1998.

International migration has remained absolutely stationary during 2003-2011. The number of return emigrants was 8.9 lakh in 2003 and stood at 11.5 lakh in 2011. The number of non-resident Keralites was 27.3 lakh in 2003 and stood at 34.4 lakh in 2011. Migration rates, however, experienced some significant decline. The emigration rate declined from 26.7 per 100 households in 2003 to 24.5 per 100 households in 2007 and then increased to 29.1 per 100 households in 2011. The corresponding decline in return emigration rate has been from 13.0 per 100 households to 11.7 per 100 households and then increasing to 14.7 per 100 households for the same period. The rate of non-resident Keralites (NRKs) per 100 households declined from 39.7 to 36.2 and then increased to 43.7 per 100 households during the same period.

Three-fourths of the Kerala households are yet to send out migrants outside India. And this situation has not undergone any change in the recent years. Gulf migration from Kerala is not as widespread among Kerala households as it is often depicted to be in the media. However, the northern districts of Kerala are gaining importance as new areas of emigration. As the years pass, more and more Kerala emigrants emanate from districts such as Malappuram, Kannur and Kasaragod. In Malappuram, 71 percent of the households have in them either an emigrant or a return emigrant each. District-wise number of emigrants in Kerala is given in Table 11.4.

Out-migration (OMI) from Kerala to other states in India has registered a significant decline, not only in terms of the rate as in the case of external migration, but also in absolute numbers. OMI declined from 11.2 lakh in 2003 to 8.7 lakh in 2007 and then increased to 9.30 lakh in 2011. OMI per 100 households declined from 16.2 in 2003 to 11.5 in 2007 and then to 11.9 in 2011. Return out-migration (ROM) registered a small increase in absolute numbers but declined in terms of the rate, from 14.4 per 100 households in 2003 to 14.0 in 2007 and then had a sharp declining trend to 6.5 in 2011.

Labour migration from India has been slowly changing

over the last few decades; whereas the 1970s and 1980s saw a large outflow of Indian workers to the Middle East, since the 1990s, a new wave of labour migration has been of highly skilled migrants, particularly of those working in the IT sector. However, the impact of growing number of foreign firms investing in India together with saturation of IT job market in the developed countries has brought about unprecedented opportunities in the country.

Table: 11.4: District-wise Number of Emigrants in Kerala during 2011

Districts	Return Emigrants	Emigrants	Non-Resident Keralites	Out-migration
Thiruvanantha-Puram	196101	229732	425833	44382
Kollam	116927	167446	284373	76161
Pathanamthitta	15297	91381	106678	25069
Alappuzha	54688	144386	199074	101331
Kottayam	11846	117460	129306	64247
Idukki	6738	7690	14428	20752
Ernakulum	62312	136113	198425	82498
Thrissur	149132	198368	347500	90425
Palakkad	83388	142020	225408	189346
Malappuram	154122	408884	563006	44165
Kozhikode	114424	206719	321143	48332
Wayanad	14489	26874	41363	19390
Kannur	125303	283045	408348	81770
Kasaragod	45580	120425	166005	42856
Kerala	1150347	2280543	3430890	930724

Source: Kerala Migration Survey, 2011, CDS,

11.3 Kudumbashree (The Poverty Eradication Mission)

Kudumbashree (etymological meaning being, prosperity of the family), the women-oriented, community-based poverty alleviation programme, based on micro credit and self-help groups is being implemented in Kerala by the state government, with the active support of Government of India and NABARD to cure the morbid development imbalances in the state. Its mission statement is "to eradicate absolute poverty in ten years through concerted community action under the leadership of local self-government, by facilitating organization of the poor, combining self-help with demand-led convergence of available services and resources to tackle the multiple dimensions and manifestation of poverty, holistically". It aims at removing poverty among rural women households, besides empowering the women, by forming self-help groups and encouraging their entrepreneurial or other wide range activities.

The purpose of the mission is to ensure that the women should no longer remain as passive recipients of public assistance, but rather as active leaders for further development initiatives. Kerala is witnessing a silent revolution—spawning women power, possibly restoring to the state its lost matriarchal legacy, where the women enjoyed pre-eminence, safety, security and respected, including self-respect. This female empowerment is taking place through the Kudumbashree movement, which has engulfed the state. Thrift and credit societies, linkage banking, lease land farming, rural micro enterprises etc. are some of the initiatives introduced by Kudumbashree to improve the livelihood of the poor women in the neighbourhood groups.

In Kerala, Kudumbashree is playing a critical role in the implementation of the National Rural Employment Guarantee Scheme. IHD (2008) found that innovative implementation mechanisms like vesting the responsibility of implementation in Kudumbashree (self-help groups) in Kerala are illustrative of the space available for effective implementation of MGNREGA, and especially that of women's participation.

11.4 MGNREGA in Kerala

This scheme could have been welcomed enthusiastically as

a boon to Kerala in the background of the realities related to poverty, low work participation rate of women, unemployment and the concerns over ecology, water resources and agriculture. In Kerala, the programme was initiated in February 2006 in the rural areas of two districts—Palakkad and Wayanad. The programme was extended to Kasaragod and Idukki by February, 2007 in second phase and to the remaining 10 districts by January 2009 in third phase. This programme came to be known as Kerala State Rural Employment Guarantee Scheme. The Government of Kerala issued detailed guidelines for the implementation of MGNREGA. The responsibility was assigned primarily to local-self-governments. In Kerala, there are elected village councils (*gram panchayats*) for an average population of 30,000.

The agglomeration of few neighbouring *gram panchayats* (GPs) is called a block panchayat. For each revenue district, there is an elected district council (district panchayat). Thus, there is a three-tier system of local-self-government, each one with specific functions and responsibilities. The implementation of scheme through panchayat in close association with the Kudumbashree system has been one of the defining features of MGNREGA implementation in the state. Kerala has one of the highest unemployment rates in the country. But most of the unemployed are educated. Thus, MGNREGA has only a limited application in tackling the problem of unemployment among the poor of Kerala. Vijayanand (2009) pointed out the salient features of the MGNREGA in Kerala as under:

1. Implementation of MGNREGA through *gram panchayat*.
2. Communicating the distinctive features of the scheme to the various stakeholders, especially to panchayat leaders.
3. Involvement of Kudumbashree network of poor women in a big way.
4. Focus on total resource management in forest areas, river basins and watershed areas as the state has very little public land.

5. Designing processes and programmes to see that MGNREGA fits into the administrative operating system, now existing in *panchayat*.
6. Institution of consistent and coherent information and accountability systems and participatory processes to ensure transparency.
7. Aim of zero corruption in implementing MGNREGA.

11.5 Implementation Mechanism and Basic Issues of MGNREGA in Kerala

The Kerala Rural Employment Guarantee Scheme (KREGS) was introduced in June 2006, even though the scheme was formally inaugurated on 2nd of February, 2002 in Pattambi in Palakkad district. The state government constituted a State Employment Guarantee Council with a chairperson to advise the state government on all matters concerning the scheme and its implementation—determine preferred work, review the monitoring and redressal mechanisms, promote dissemination of information about this Act and scheme and prepare annual report to be laid before the State Legislature. The Rural Development Department is the nodal agency for implementing the Act.

The rural development commissioner is the nodal officer for implementation of MGNREGA at the state level. At the district level, the district collector is the nodal officer. A district project officer with necessary staff is appointed to assist the district collector. The district programme coordinator shall constitute a committee at the district level with the following members for the smooth implementation of the scheme, namely, district programme co-ordinator as its chairman and joint programme co-ordinator as its convener. The other members of committee would be project officer DRDA, deputy director of panchayat, district labour officer, principal agriculture officer, district soil conservation officer, district mission coordinator Kudumbashree, divisional forest officers, lead district manager, tribal development officer/P.O ITDP, assistant development commissioner, assistant project officer (SM), and any such other official decided by the district programme co-ordinator.

At the block panchayat level, a block programme officer of the rank of block panchayat secretary has been appointed to coordinate the scheme at the three levels of *panchayat* and its implementation. At the *gram panchayat* level, an overseer or assistant engineer and an accountant-cum-computer operator are appointed to assist the *gram panchayat* and its secretary. The programme will be implemented through the panchayati raj institutions (PRIs) namely *gram panchayat*, block panchayat and district panchayat in the ratio 50:30:20. The *gram sabha* is the statutorily mandated institutional mechanism for community participation.

The Act authorizes the *gram sabha* to recommend works to be taken up under the scheme, to monitor and supervise these works and to conduct social audits of the implementation.

According to Pratap Singh (2009), *gram sabha* has to play a very crucial role in implementing MGNREGA, especially in three important stages in the process of MGNREGA viz.: (i) preparation of shelf of projects; (ii) appraisal of shelf of projects; and (iii) conducting of social audit. These activities are very essential for the effective implementation of MGNREGA, which necessarily warrant convening the meeting of the *gram sabha*. There are instances where *gram sabha* meetings were not convened in certain areas of the district in certain states.

The *gram panchayat* is responsible for all other works related to planning and implementation. The block panchayat is responsible for planning at the block level, and for monitoring and supervision. District panchayat is responsible for finalizing the district plans for MGNREGA, which is a comprehensive plan of action for the scheme for the district, and its monitoring and supervision. As per MGNREGA, a perspective plan has to be made and should be discussed and approved with modifications suggested by *gram sabha* at the *gram*, block and district level panchayats. The annual plan is worked out from this perspective plan. The demand for work, the nature and time of work and preference is decided by those who are likely to seek employment.

A number of micro level organizations are involved in the formulation and implementation of MGNREGA programme at the panchayat level which are given a central role in the planning and implementation of MGNREGA and are the sole agencies responsible for implementation of local development projects under the scheme in Kerala. The panchayat governing council, which has been strengthened by the decentralized planning introduced in Kerala since 1996, has a pivotal role to play in the smooth functioning of MGNREGA. It is the *gram panchayat* that takes a leading role in publicizing the novel programme among people. At the panchayat level, MGNREGA was given publicity by means of processions, distribution of pamphlets, awareness classes and *gram sabhas*. Kudumbashree is a women's organization working under a state level poverty alleviation programme. It reaches to all households in the panchayat through neighbour hood groups (NHGs).

In each ward, the NHGs are grouped in to an area development society (ADS). At the panchayat level, the Kudumbashree activities are managed by the community development society (CDS), elected from among the ADS. Involvement of Kudumbashree is one of the most important aspects that makes the programme in Kerala unique. Planning starts from NHG and it moves up to the panchayat governing body. The process of implementation begins from panchayat and ADS becomes the lowest tier to mobilize workers and supervise the work at which they are entrusted with the role of supervision, distribution of implements, marking of attendance in NMR, etc. It would be incomplete unless and until Kudumbashree plays it role in the implementation of MGNREGA.

At the other end of the scale, there are some surprises.

Kerala is at the rock bottom, but perhaps this is partly a reflection of the low demand for MGNREGA employment in Kerala, rather than of a failure to provide. The same interpretation, however, is unlikely to apply to Maharashtra and West Bengal. The fact that MGNREGA is a flop in both states may seem surprising, but it is actually in line with recent policy priorities. There is another way of looking at the state as is well known; the southern and western states (Andhra Pradesh, Gujarat, Karnataka, Kerala, Maharashtra and Tamil Nadu) routinely do better than most of the northern and eastern states when it comes to social policy and rural development programmes. The large north Indian states, for their part, tend to lag far behind. But when it comes to MGNREGA, the pattern is reversed: only one of the southern or western states (Karnataka) has generated more than 10 person-days of employment per rural household in 2006-07, while the eastern and northern states have done comparatively well in this respect. Of course, this pattern has to be read in the light of the fact that the need for fall-back employment may be greater in the eastern and northern regions.

From the various studies regards the implementation of MGNREGA in the state of Kerala, it seems that while the programme is being implemented in letter, the spirit of the scheme seems to be missing. The programme falls short of its objective of guaranteeing minimum100 days of employment to each family, with the average number of days of work through MGNREGA being just 20 per household. To the extent this goal is not fulfilled, it may not be called a successful programme in Kerala. Further, the financial ramifications also need to be analyzed. Since the average number of days of work through MGNREGA is about 20 days per worker, it needs to be explored as to what happens to wages that are slotted for the worker for the remaining 80 days of work.

The reasons for the underperformance in achieving this vital objective need to be studied. On the positive side, one feature, which stands out in the implementation of

MGNREGA in the State, is the overwhelming participation of women in the programme. The share of women in the number of person days generated was 85.01 percent in 2006-07 which rose to 93.36 percent in 2012-13 in the state, which is way above the work participation rate of women in the state. This could well be one of the biggest votaries in support of the programme as the wages in the hands of the women get translated into useful investments in the form of education for the children and asset creation for the household.

Considering the overall performance of the MGNREGA in the state, it is argued that the scheme is yet to pick up in its full swing. There are several constraints which hinder the effective implementation, like difficulty in identification of sufficient number of projects, lack of staff at *gram panchayat* level, lack of participation of male members, lack of provisions for undertaking schemes requiring material and skilled labour cost, lack of awareness among various stakeholders, lack of capacity among the supervisors, reluctance in collaborating with the NGOs in the state, lack of cooperation and collaboration between the project staff and panchayat functionaries at various levels and lack of interest among the elected representatives etc.

Moreover, the topography, climatic conditions, rural employment market, literacy level, infrastructure development, rural employment market, wage rate of unskilled labourers especially for men, work culture etc. in Kerala does not make the scheme so attractive, as in other states. Creation of durable assets requires higher percentage of material and skilled labour cost. There are many essential areas outside the priority areas prescribed in Schedule I of the Act, like agriculture sector in Kerala which requires attention and investment for the progress of the rural areas as well as improvement of livelihood of rural folk. The state government should take up the matter with the Central government and get the Schedule I modified to suit the Kerala situation.

Despite high levels of unemployment in Kerala, the high

levels of literacy mean that unemployed men are educated and even though many men signed up initially and had job cards made, they do not want to do unskilled manual work and therefore have not applied for work under the scheme. While women too are educated, they have not felt it to be below their dignity and in fact women frequently said that MGNREGA work, being 'government work', gave them a higher status. Thus, because of this problem of statuesque, educated people are unwilling to participate in the kind of jobs provided under MGNREGA. Another problem related to unsuccessful implementation of MGNREGA is that it provides very low wages as compared to other occupations in the state except in some tribal and backward regions. In Kerala, most of the jobs fetch ₹ 300-500 per day, while MGNREGA provides half of it.

If implemented properly, MGNREGA would have considerable impacts on the social, economic and political arena of the rural community. It would protect rural households from poverty and hunger. The availability of employment at the local area would also lead to reduction of migration. It would ensure gender equality and social justice by offering the job to all adults, irrespective of their caste and creed, age, economic status/position and equal wages to all for the same work. Every rupee paid under wages would directly reach the hands of the workers. The availability of money and its circulation at the local level will boost up the local economy.

The in-built mechanism of monitoring and social audit will help reduce corruption and malpractices and ensure transparency and accountability. The scheme may also help in creating social assets to a certain extent. After all, MGNREGA should be viewed not only as a scheme for employment guarantee but also as an effective process of promoting citizen's active engagement and commitment in creating social assets in improving their living conditions at the local level.

11.6 Role of Kudumbashree in MGNREGA Implementation

In Kerala, Kudumbashree is playing a critical role in the

implementation of the National Rural Employment Guarantee Scheme. Not only are women accessing the scheme in much larger proportions in all districts than the stipulated percentage (almost 80 percent of the workers in the scheme are women), Kudumbashree groups are active in implementing the scheme with women 'mates' with the responsibility of overall supervision. Kudumbashree and panchayats have been very vigilant in spreading awareness about MGNREGA through radio, posters, television, notice boards of *gram sabhas*, etc. The manifold functions taken up by Kudumbashree members range from identification of projects to supervision of works and submission of records for wage disbursement. This arrangement has two positive aspects, namely: (i) since Kudumbashree has grass root level reach through NHGs, the projects identified by them would reflect the needs and requirements of the people, and (ii) the involvement of women in MGNREGA is a capacity building process for them.

Women have been organized into self-help groups known as Kudumbashree groups. These engage in micro enterprises of various kinds. This offers an alternative to agricultural work but since the state government has placed Kudumbashree in charge of managing MGNREGA, women have easily been directed into this work. A feature of the MGNREGA specific to Kerala is that the sites are managed by women and that most of the women coming for work have already been mobilized into self-help groups, so that there was prior experience of working together and already existing female managerial capacity, both of which help to make MGNREGA more accessible to women.

The Kerala state government has entrusted the line management and implementation of the MGNREGA to Kudumbashree (the state poverty eradication mission and a programme that has mobilized women into self-help groups for economic activity). The Mission statement of Kudumbashree (1999) reads as follows: "To eradicate absolute poverty in 10 years through concerted community action under the leadership of local governments, by facilitating organizations of the poor for combining self-help with demand led convergence of available services and resources to tackle the multiple dimensions and manifestations of poverty, holistically".

11.7 Neighbourhood Groups (NHGs)/Ayalkoottam

Neighbourhood group is an association of 20 to 40 women members, belonging to high risk families. They elect women from among themselves as resident community volunteers and another one is selected as president of the NHG and the three others are selected as community volunteers, each of whom has specific responsibilities viz., health, infrastructure creation and income generation. They are, therefore, designated as community health volunteers, community infrastructure volunteers and community income generating volunteers.

The community health volunteer is responsible for all the health related activities of the NHG like immunization, maternal care, child care, nutrition and propagation of ideas like cleanliness, hygiene, etc. The community infrastructure volunteer is in charge of the basic infrastructure needs of the NHGs such as housing, sanitation, drinking water, drainage, etc. The community income generation activity volunteer looks after the income generating activities of the NHG. She has to identify all potential agencies, departments and organizations to be engaged in promotion of self-employment activities. She also liaisons with the National Bank for Agriculture and Rural Development and commercial banks on behalf of the NHG. Proper training and orientation are given to the above volunteers in their respective areas. Each NHG prepares an action plan on the basis of the needs of the member households of the NHG and such plans are called micro plan of the NHGs.

11.8 Area Development Societies (ADSs)

Area development societies at the ward level are formed of 20-35 NHGs and the five member committee of the all the NHGs constitutes the governing body of the ADS, which provides a volunteer area development supervisor (ADS), who is placed in charge of the MGNREGA work and ensures proper maintenance of muster rolls and provision of work-site facilities. The ADS is usually the head of an existing self-help group, and an emergent village leader. She looks after two or three sites, depending on the size of the village.

Typically, a woman between 30 and 45 years, the ADS is educated, and has been associated with Kudumbashree for a few years. One ADS described her MGNREGA responsibilities as follows: 'My responsibility includes visiting panchayat office and looking for work, collect estimates of the work, fill forms for members and collect them, give job card and account books...give forms to panchayat, collect muster rolls, provide water at worksite, shelter, and keep an *ayah* if there are small kids'. The ADS has a chairperson, a vice-chairperson and 7 other members. The community organizer of the municipality acts as the member secretary of the ADS. The ADS integrates the micro plans of the NHGs and after discussion and scrutiny, a consolidated action plan is prepared and is known as mini plan.

By giving the responsibility of MGNREGA implementation to Kudumbashree, the state government has further consolidated the position of this programme for women. Field work has shown that there is a perception among women that one needs to be a member of Kudumbashree in order to work on MGNREGA sites. However, this is not the case. But women are joining up to make sure of getting work. Roles and responsibilities of ADS prepared by KILA (2008) for MGNREGA booklet are as follows:

1. The estimates of the work should be displayed on the board. Number of people working on that day, number of implements used and cost should be mentioned in the board. They should provide all the essentials to the workers.
2. Provide tools/implements at the worksite and return it back without any damage and see to that they are used carefully.
3. Get signatures of the workers in the muster roll before

starting the day's work and at the end of each day in the presence of everyone.

4. Muster roll should be closed every week and handed over to the panchayat. The daily attendance should be intimated to the secretary, *gram panchayat*.
5. ADS should ensure that the workers are coming on time and doing the correct amount of work. She should make the lazy ones work and if they disobey, give the details of such workers to the *gram panchayat* secretary.
6. ADS should make sure the measurement of the work to be done at the site and finish it within the stipulated time and date.
7. Site diary to be maintained, giving details of income and expense, number of implements used; number of people and days worked by each one. A copy of the same should be handed over to the secretary, once in two weeks.
8. If there are children below 5 years, a shed to be made and an *ayah* to look after the children.
9. First aid box to be provided at the worksite and if needed the injured to be taken to the hospital.
10. Interact with the panchayat and other officials and ensure that the work is done without any hindrance.
11. Ensure that the wages are given on time.

Though designed well, lack of adequate training in conceptualizing watershed development programme, supervision of works and maintenance of records has placed the Kudumbashree office bearers in a difficult position. If they are given proper training in conceptualizing the programme and implementation, more innovative projects can be identified and implemented.

11.9 Community Development Society (CDS)

Community development society is the apex body at the town level and is the coordinating agency for programme implementation. Chairperson, vice chairperson and members of all the ADSs form the general body of the community development society (CDS). A project officer of the municipality acts as the member Secretary of the community development society. The community development society has a president, vice president and seven other members elected from the general body of the CDS to form the committee of the CDS. The committee and the member secretary constitute the governing body of the CDS. The community development society monitors the programmes undertaken by the ADSs on monthly basis and takes steps to improve the implementation of the programmes. Various developmental programmes initiated under community development society and the area development societies include training programme for women to start income generating units, water supply, conduct of health education camps, construction of dual pit latrines, undertaking micro enterprises, rising of pathways and cultural programmes, etc.

Kudumbashree became the lifeline to many of the poor women in the state of Kerala. Resultantly, the women of the state have become active participants in the planning and implementation process of various anti poverty programmes like MGNREGA. By participating in various income generating-cum-developmental activities, the morale and confidence of women have become very high. Women who were regarded as voiceless and powerless, started identifying their inner power, their strength, opportunities for growth and their role in reshaping their own destiny.

At the level of personal space—both mental and physical—there has been a tremendous expansion for women, through both an enormous and rapid increase of knowledge, awareness and skills in new areas, as well as through the expansion of institutional space, which has opened up a new and hitherto unknown world to women. Women's larger role in decision-making seems to be resented by men, even though they did not say so directly, but hinted at it indirectly, giving a different reason. In the public arena, participation in public life and social prestige and esteem were seen to be closely linked. The first has made women "visible" on a large scale in the public domain as never before and they are admired for it, publicly.

To go any further, structural changes are needed and it will become necessary for women to engage with "strategic" and "transformative" issues like unequal control over property and other productive assets, opportunities for employment, equal wages and a level playing field in the market. Women would have to enter the public decision-making forums and lobby for women-friendly policies, even in such basic matters such as support services for women workers.

11.10 Employment Generation through MGNREGA

India has a long history and experience in implementing wage employment programmes. Giving a statutory framework to wage employment programmes—based on the experience of these programmes, the National Rural Employment Guarantee Act (NREGA) was enacted to reinforce the commitment towards livelihood security in rural areas. The Act was notified on 7th September, 2005 in which the ongoing programmes of Sampoorna Grameen Rozgar Yojana (SGRY-2001) and National Food for Work Programme (NFFWP-2004) were subsumed within the scheme. These wage employment programmes implemented by State governments with Central assistance were self-targeting, and the objective was to provide enhanced livelihood security, especially of those dependent on casual manual labour.

The significance of MGNREGA lies in the fact that it creates a right-based framework for wage employment programmes and makes the government legally accountable for providing employment to those who ask for it. In this way, the legislation goes beyond providing a social safety net towards guaranteeing the right to employment. It is a first ever law internationally, that guarantees wage employment at an unprecedented scale with the objective of strengthening natural resource management through works that address cause of chronic poverty like drought, deforestation and soil erosion and hence encourages sustainable development. The process outcomes include strengthening grass root process of democracy and infusing transparency and accountability in governance. It was implemented in a various phases. In phase one, it was implemented in 200 backward districts of the country, additional 130 districts in phase two in 2007-08 and the remaining 266 districts were notified in September 2008 and the scheme has now been extended to all the districts of the country.

In Kerala, the program was initiated in February 2006 in the rural areas of two districts viz. Palakkad and Wayanad. The programme was extended to Kasaragod and Idukki by February, 2007 in second phase and to the remaining 10 districts by January 2009 in the third phase. This programme came to be known as a Kerala State Rural Employment Guarantee Scheme. The Government of Kerala has issued detailed guidelines for implementing MGNREGA. The responsibility has been assigned primarily to local-self governments. In Kerala, there are elected village councils (*gram panchayats*) for an average population of thirty thousand. The agglomeration of a few neighbouring *gram panchayats* (GPs) is called a block panchayat. For each revenue district, there is an elected district council (district panchayat). Thus, there is a three-tier system of local self- government, each one with specific functions and responsibilities. Kerala has one of the highest unemployment rates in the country. But most of the unemployed are educated. Thus, MGNREGA has only limited application in tackling the problem of unemployment among the poor of Kerala. Vijayanand pointed out the salient features of the MGNREGA in Kerala, which are as under:

1. Implementation of NREGA through *gram panchayats*.
2. Communicating the distinctive features of the scheme to the various stakeholders, especially to panchayat leaders.
3. Involvement of Kudumbasree network of poor women in a big way.
4. Focus on total resource management in forest areas, river

basins and watershed areas as the state has very little public land.

5. Designing processes and programmes to see that MGNREGA fits into the administrative operating system, now existing in Panchayats.
6. Institution of consistent and coherent information and accountability systems and participatory processes to ensure transparency.
7. An aim for zero corruption in implementing MGNREGA.

In the state of Kerala, the performance is good when we take the indicator of providing employment as against employment demand which has increased from 94.45 percent in 2006-07 to 99.84 percent in 2009-10 and further to 99.90 percent in 2012-13. But the problem in Kerala is different in the sense that Kerala's problem of unemployment is of educated people rather than the involuntary. As people are educated, they are reluctant to do unskilled manual work provided under MGNREGA. Whenever people hear about MGNREGA, they register under the scheme, but half of the registered household do not demand the job.

We can understand that the number of households registered for job has increased sharply from 2.14 lakh in 2006-07 to 32.56 lakh in 2011-12 and further to 24.86 lakh in 2012-13. But the actual demand for employment has increased from 1.04 lakh during 2006-07 to 16.71 lakh during 2012-13, while the employment provided has increased from 1.99 lakh (94.45 percent) to 16.70 lakh (99.90 percent) during the same period recording manifold increase over a period of seven years. Thus, it may be stated that the scheme has been successful in providing employment to all those who demanded employment through the scheme.

The districts-wise analysis is shown in Table 11.6. The scale of registrations in Wayanad and Palakkad, the two districts where the MGNREGA was first introduced in the state, came as a big surprise for most observers. In Kerala, in the first phase of implementation in Wayanad and Palakkad, the share of employment offered in 2006-07 was only 94.10 percent of the household demand. However, by the next year (2007-08), the proportion of demand met, increased to 96.63 percent which includes two more districts (Kasaragod and Idukki) and during this period in Palakkad district, whatever households demanded, 100 percent employment was provided and became one of the best districts of the country in the implementation of MGNREGA and by 2008-09 and onwards, the scheme was able to offer employment to almost all the households and persons that demanded employment which includes almost all the districts of Kerala. The case is similar in case of actual employment provided as a share of employment offered—the coverage has been almost hundred percent. Almost all the households who were offered employment, were actually provided employment as well (Table 11.5).

Table: 11.5: Employment Provided over Employment Demanded: District-wise Analysis (in percent)

Districts	2007-08	2008-09	2009-10	2010-11	2011-12	2012-13
Palakkad	100	100	100	98.70	99.96	99.97
Wayanad	99.92	99.62	100	97.01	99.89	99.98
Idukki	88.85	99.76	99.96	99.15	99.98	99.97
Kasaragod	84.52	97.25	99.98	99.03	99.97	99.95
Alappuzha		98.30	100	97.78	99.86	99.94
Ernakulum		99.64	99.04	98.94	99.94	99.98
Kannur		99.27	99.51	98.77	99.84	99.93
Kollam		94.45	99.57	97.33	99.8	99.95
Kottayam		97.86	99.66	98.55	99.84	99.95
Kozhikode		98.87	99.87	98.78	99.84	99.96
Malappuram		99.78	99.93	99.03	99.81	99.95
Pathanam-thitta		97.49	99.91	97.93	99.96	99.95
Thrissur		99.50	99.78	99.36	99.74	99.93
Thiruvanan-thapuram		99.94	100	97.65	99.95	99.98
Grand Total	96.63	99.04	99.84	98.41	99.88	99.96

Source: www.nrega.nic.in

When the MGNREGA was first introduced in 2006, there was a widespread belief that the scheme, though of great potential benefit for other states in the country, was of little relevance to Kerala. This is because Kerala is facing the problem of jobless growth with an unemployment of 83.45 lakh people (25 percent). From the above analysis, we find that with unemployment of 83.45 lakh people, only 32.56 lakh households registered and the actual demand for employment was only 11.75 lakh households. This means that MGNREGA was unable to solve the problem of unemployment in Kerala or people were reluctant to provide their labour service.

Kerala is facing the problem of educated unemployment and they are highly skilled labours and are unwilling to undertake the jobs created by MGNREGA which provides unskilled manual work for rural people. The mental attitude and statuesque of educated Keralites do not allow them to take-up such work. Another problem is related with the wage rates provided under MGNREGA—even if the wage rate increased to ₹ 164 under the scheme, it is too low as compared with the market wage rate in Kerala which varies between ₹ 300-500. Since educated unemployment requires the creation of skilled jobs rather than unskilled manual jobs, MGNREGA was considered inappropriate and irrelevant for Kerala for solving the problem of unemployment.

11.11 Women Participation and Empowerment through MGNREGA

Women participation during the scheme execution in Kerala has been very high, considering the provisions of earmarking a minimum of 33 percent of employment generated to them. Significantly, Kudumbashree volunteers (all women) are assigned with the task of work supervisors at the worksites. This resulted in improving their managerial, technical and soft skills, marginally. No gender consideration seems to have been adopted in the districts for providing work site facilities. Provision of keeping a maid for looking after children below 5 years of age at the worksite was rarely seen in the state. Mostly the workers used to keep the children at home itself, under the custody of aged relatives.

Presence of women work supervisors was also a positive factor in attracting more women workers in various ways. Strict adherence to the norms of equal wages for men and women, probably for the first time in the history of implementation of wage employment programmes in Kerala, has resulted in improving the attractability of scheme among women. The studies done by the scholars like Narayanan (2008) and Vijayanand (2009), show that in spite of many limitations, MGNREGA has become a women's programme. Narayanan and Vijayanand have restricted their study to one state only, but Sharif (2008) has studied seven states. Their common conclusion is that the Act had a positive impact on women's employment opportunities and intra-household bargaining power. It is an interesting fact that the female work participation rate is in general below 18 percent in the state of Kerala. However, on the MGNREGA worksite, their participation rate is more than 90 percent.

Table 11.6 shows the district-wise analysis of women participation in Kerala which has increased from 65.31 percent in 2006-07 to 92.95 percent in 2012-2013. The percentage of women participation has increased in each and every district and is the highest in Kottayam district where women participation is 96.69 percent, followed by Alappuzha (96.33 percent), Thrissur (96.21 percent), Ernakulum (95.80 percent), and the lowest participation was in Idukki (77.08 percent) in the year of 2012-13.

The low and declining participation of women in the district of Idukki is mainly due to their tea plantations. In the early period of implementation, their participation is comparatively better because they had higher wages under the scheme than the wage rate under tea plantation factory. But when the workers from tea plantation shifted to the scheme, the wage rate in the tea plantation sector was raised and made more than the MGNREGA wage rate. That is why, they again went for tea plantations. And also, tea plantation is their hereditary job where women are the main workers; they are reluctant to give up their jobs. But in most of the districts of Kerala, workers, especially women under MGNREGA, are new entrants to the labour market.

Table: 11.6: Percentage of Women Participation in Kerala (District-wise Analysis)

Districts	2007-08	2008-09	2009-10	2010-11	2011-12	2012-13
Palakkad	83.00	89.07	92.21	93.25	95.65	95.56
Wayanad	59.00	76.60	79.44	84.93	86.43	86.83
Idukki	79.10	87.06	72.54	71.79	76.92	77.08
Kasaragod	79.45	82.79	87.85	87.4	92.09	93.07
Alappuzha		89.45	93.28	94.45	96.13	96.33
Ernakulum		91.08	93.93	94.69	95.69	95.80
Kannur		85.81	93.58	95.49	95.53	95.83
Kollam		82.53	87.18	86.9	91.58	91.9
Kottayam		85.84	94.58	95.54	96.42	96.69
Kozhikode		83.34	92.71	93.68	95.11	95.51
Malappuram		78.79	92.26	92.86	92.94	92.66
Pathanam-Thitta		82.08	92.89	94.65	95.55	95.42
Thrissur		94.44	95.87	95.64	96.33	96.21
Thiruvandram		85.02	90.02	90.87	94.2	94.45
Grand Total	72.55	85.01	88.19	90.36	92.85	92.95

Source: www.nrega.nic.in

Implementation of MGNREGA has contributed to very high levels of women empowerment. As the work is organized by women's groups, the gender perspective gets built in automatically. A feature of MGNREGA specific to Kerala is that the site is managed by women and that most of the women who come for work have already been mobilized under SHGs—so that there was a prior experience of working together and already the female managerial capacity existed, helping them to make MGNREGA more accessible to the women. For the first time, equal wages are really paid and this has boosted the earnings of women. As the wages are paid into bank accounts, the habit of thrift which was already inculcated through the Kudumbashree experiment has further been strengthened. As the bank deposits are increasing, the intra-household status of the women has also been improving commensurately as she now controls substantial cash resources and withdrawal can be only on her decision.

There are various explanations for the varying participation of women workers under the MGNREGA. Factors that have encouraged women workers' participation include the nature of the job not requiring special knowledge and skill (Krishnaraj et al., 2004); out-migration of male family members (Bhatty, 2006; Mehrotra, 2008; Talukdar, 2008); the employment opportunity being available at the doorstep (Khera and Nayak, 2009); a tradition of rural women working in others' fields; the provision of equal, non-discriminatory wages (ibid); and innovative experiments in implementation like the female mate system in Rajasthan (Khera, 2008), synergisation of MGNREGA with Kudumbashree in Kerala (Vijayakumar and Thomas, 2008), and in Bihar, gender differential tasks for uniform (minimum) wages (Pankaj, 2008a). Thus, empowerment of rural women is an unintending consequence of MGNREGA.

Moreover, actual performance of MGNREGA in Kerala owes much in terms of women participation better than any other states especially because of the state government commitment and the advanced managerial role of Kudumbashree and area development supervisor in particular which mobilize, coordinate and manage the women workers under the scheme.

11.12 Participation of SCs and STs

If we analyze across the states, the highest SC participation was in Punjab (78.27 percent), followed by Haryana (52.21 percent), Uttar Pradesh (33.75) and West Bengal (32.95 percent) with lowest participation of SCs in the states like Assam (5.70 percent), Gujarat (8.99 percent), Kerala (15.26), Maharashtra (16.93 percent), and Karnataka (16.95 percent) during the year 2012-13. Thus, MGNREGA provides a solution for inclusive growth by providing legal guarantee to the employment for under-privileged sections of the society in the country (Table 11.7).

Table: 11.7: Participation of SCs under MGNREGA in Kerala (in percent)

Districts	2006-07	2007-08	2008-09	2009-10	2010-11	2011-12	2012-13
Palakkad	29.41	21.09	27.84	23.95	23.92	28.04	31.25
Wayanad	8.06	5.83	6.04	6.35	6.27	3.8	3.81
Idukki		19.31	20.31	11.08	10.69	10.96	10.31
Kasaragod		6.92	10.36	8.62	6.36	5.17	4.45
Alappuzha			18.88	15.79	15.29	11.72	11.29
Ernakulum			16.83	19.09	17.9	14.07	14.74
Kannur			2.11	3.21	2.79	6.47	2.69
Kollam			18.9	12.73	11.66	2.8	10.42
Kottayam			13.24	14.33	13.24	11.41	11.19
Kozhikode			20.86	15.85	16.05	8.36	13.65
Malappuram			34.36	32.86	32.22	11.99	30.13
Pathanamthitta			28.71	27.25	27.72	29.88	21.3
Thrissur			34.87	28.01	26.77	10.18	31.82
Thiruvanantha-Puram			18.57	14.54	14.44	23.98	9.93
Grand Total	20.1	14.76	19.47	16.77	17.04	14.31	15.26

Source: www.nrega.nic.in

As far as participation of SCs in Kerala is concerned, it has been fluctuating over a period of time. It was 20.1 percent in 2006-07, which reduced to 14.76 percent in the next year and then increased to and was the highest in 2008-09 i.e. 19.47 percent and since then, there has been declining trend. If we look at district-wise profile of participation of SCs, we can see that Palakkad district was the highest with a share of 22.65 percent in 2006-07 which increased to 31.25 percent, followed by Thrissur, Malappuram, Thiruvananthapuram. The lowest participation was in Kannur, Kasaragod and Wayanad.

Kerala is also the home for indigenous tribal population who constitute 1.14 percent of the total population. Major portion of them reside in the main stream with other people. The highest concentration of scheduled tribes is seen in Wayanad district (37.36 percent) followed by Idukki (14 percent) and Palakkad (10.89 percent) and these three districts together account for over 60 percent of ST population of the state. The coastal district of Alappuzha has the lowest percentage of the tribal population (Table 11.8).

As far as tribal people are concerned, they were concentrated in Wayanad district with 22.94 percent in 2006-07, and increased to the highest level of 27.98 percent in 2007-08, then reached to 26.81, 27.21, 23.33, 18.12 and 18.85 percent respectively in subsequent years followed by Idukki, Palakkad and Kasaragod. The lowest participation was found in Alappuzha, Kollam, Thrissur and other districts.

However, this decline of SC and ST participation in the state of Kerala under the MGNREGA does not mean an actual reduction of their participation. Because the scheme was initially introduced in Palakkad and Wayanad districts of Kerala where there is maximum number of SC and ST population, so when the Act was introduced, initially there was a higher degree of their participation. Later the scheme was introduced in the remaining districts of Kerala, where proportion of SC and ST participation to total creation of employment days under MGNREGA had come down.

Table: 11.8: Participation of STs under MGNREGA in Kerala
(in percent)

Districts	2006-07	2007-08	2008-09	2009-10	2010-11	2011-12	2012-13
Palakkad	4.23	6.87	4.93	5.00	7.03	4.22	5.24
Wayanad	22.94	27.98	26.81	27.21	23.33	18.12	18.85
Idukki		11.48	17.84	8.61	7.37	6.74	7.29
Kasaragod		5.82	7.8	4.71	4.83	2.53	2.52
Alappuzha			0.06	0.42	0.45	0.19	0.22
Ernakulum			0.45	0.84	0.69	0.56	0.65
Kannur			5.15	4.9	4.24	3.68	3.46
Kollam			0.41	0.42	0.48	0.34	0.42
Kottayam			2.08	2.69	2.35	1.1	1.44
Kozhikode			0.7	1.15	0.96	0.55	0.87
Malappuram			1.07	1.2	1.31	0.77	0.75
Pathanamthitta			0.33	1.06	1.39	0.85	0.98
Thrissur			0.14	0.72	0.55	0.4	0.57
Thiruvanantha-Puram			6.73	1.03	1.07	0.8	0.76
Grand Total	12.39	13.03	9.26	5.33	3.44	2.37	2.59

Source: www.nrega.nic.in

Though it was widely realized that MGNREGA is not the main solution to the unemployment problem of the poor in Kerala where a large number of the poor seek not manual work but self-employment and wage employment in the formal informal sectors, at the same time, the State was able to foresee a niche for MGNREGA in reducing poverty of at least half a million poor agricultural labourer families who are expected to turn up for works under MGNREGA and get an additional annual cash income of ₹ 15,000 per annum. Like as free market economy takes care of growth, MGNREGA is a legal entitlement for employment in the economy.

References

Azeez, N.P. Abdul and Akthar, S.M. Jawed (2012), *Economy of*

Kerala: A Development Experience, Lambert Academic Publishing, Germany.

Bhat, P.N.M. and S. Irudaya Rajan (1990), "Demographic Transition in Kerala Revisited", *Economic and Political Weekly*, Vol. 20, No. 11, pp. 1547-1560.

Bhatty, Kiran (2006), "Employment Guarantee and Child Rights", *Economic and Political Weekly*, Vol. 41, No. 20, pp. 1965-1967.

Chathukulam, Jose and K. Gireesan (2007), "Impact Assessment of NREGS in Kerala: An Evaluation of Systems and Processes", Centre for Rural Management, Kottayam, September.

Government of India (2001), "National Human Development Report", Planning Commission, New Delhi.

Government of India (2002), "National Human Development Report, 2001", Planning Commission, Oxford University Press, New Delhi.

Government of Kerala (1999), "Kudumbashree for Poverty Eradication", Department of Public Relations, Thiruvananthapuram.

Government of Kerala (2001), "Economic Review", Kerala State Planning Board.

IHD (2008), "Processes, Institutions and Mechanisms of Implementation of NREGA: Impact Assessment of Bihar and Jharkhand", Institute for Human Development, New Delhi.

Kannan, K.P. (1998), "Political Economy of Labour and Development in Kerala", *Economic and Political Weekly*, Vol. 33, No. 52, December 26.

Khera, Reetika (2008), "Group Measurement of NREGA Work: The Jalore Experiment", International Conference on NREGA: Impacts and Implementation Experiences, New Delhi, 16-17, September.

Khera, Reetika and Nandini Nayak (2009), "Women Workers and Perceptions of the National Rural Employment Guarantee Act", Economic and Political Weekly, Vol. 44, No. 43, pp. 49-57.

Krishnan, T.N. (1984), "Infant Mortality in Kerala State, India: A Preliminary Analysis", UNICEF, *Assignment Children*, Vol. 65, No. 68, pp. 293-308.

Krishnaraj, Maithreyi, Divya Pandey and Aruna Kanchi (2004), "Does EGS Require Restructuring for Poverty Alleviation and Gender Equality?: Gender Concerns and Issues for Restructuring", *Economic and Political Weekly,* Vol. 39, No.

17, pp. 174-187.

Mehrotra, Santosh (2008), "NREGA Two Years On: Where Do We Go from Here?", *Economic and Political Weekly*, Vol. 43, No. 31, pp. 27-35.

Mukherjee, Chandan and T.M.T. Isaac (1991), "Study of Educated Unemployed in Kerala: Report of the Sample Survey of Registrants of Employment Exchange", Centre for Development Studies, Kerala (mimeograph).

Nag, M. (1985), "The Impact of Social and Economic Development on Mortality: Comparative Study of Kerala and West Bengal", in S.B. Halstead, J.A. Walsh, and K.S. Warren (eds.), *Good Heal that Low Cost,* Rockefeller Foundation, New York, pp. 39-46.

Nair, M.K. Sukumaran (1997), "Rural Labour Market in Kerala: Small Holder Agriculture and Labour Market Dynamics", *Economic and Political Weekly*, August 30, pp. L-45-52.

NREGS Handbook for Local Self-governments (2008), Kerala Institute of Local Administration (KILA), Mulamkunnathukavu, Thrissur.

NSSO (2001), "Employment and Unemployment Situation in India 1999-2000 (Part-I)", NSS 55th Round: July 1999-June 2000, Report No. 458, Ministry of Statistics and Programme Implementation, Government of India, New Delhi.

NSSO (2010), "Employment and Unemployment in India, 2009-10", NSS 66th Round: July 2009-June 2010, Schedule 10, Ministry of Statistics and Programme Implementation, Government of India.

Panikar, P.G.K. (1985), "Health Care System in Kerala and Its Impact on Infant Mortality" in S.B. Halstead, J.A. Walsh, and K.S. Warren (eds.), Good Health at Low Cost, Rockefeller Foundation, New York, pp. 39-46.

Panikar, P.G.K. and Soman, C.R. (1985), "Health Status of Kerala", Centre for Development Studies, Thiruvananthapuram.

Pankaj, Ashok and Rukmini Tankha (2009), "Women's Empowerment through Guaranteed Employment", *Institute for Human Development*, Delhi.

Pratap, Mahim Singh, (2009), "A Region where NREGA is a Failure', *The Hindu*, September 6.

Shiva Kumar, A.K. (1991), "UNDP's Human Development Index: A Computation for Indian States", *Economic and Political Weekly*, Vol. 26, No. 42.

Talukdar, Ratna Bharali (2008), "NREGA Shines for Tripura Women", *India Together*, 30th June.

United Nations (1975), "Poverty, Unemployment and Development: A Case of Selected Issues with Reference to Kerala", ST/ESA/29, United Nations, New York.

Vaidyanathan, A. (1994a), "Labour Use in Rural India: A Study of Spatial and Temporal Variations", in Pravin Visaria and Rakesh Basant (eds.), Non-Agricultural Employment in India: Trends and Prospects, Sage Publications, New Delhi.

Vijayakumar, B. and S.N. Thomas (2008), "Governance, Institutions and National Rural Employment Guarantee Scheme", International Conference on NREGS in India: Impacts and Implementation Experiences, New Delhi, 16-17 September.

Vijayanand, S.M. and V.N. Jitherdran (2009), "Implementation of NREGA Experience of Kerala" in NREGA: Design Process and Impact, UNDP, New Delhi, p. 220.

Zachariah, K.C. and S. Irudaya Rajan (2012), "Inflexion in Kerala's Gulf Connection: Report on Kerala's Migration Survey, 2011, Centre for Development Studies, Working Paper No. 450, September.

Zachariah, K.C. and S. Irudaya Rajan (2007), "Economic and Social Dynamics of Migration in Kerala, 1999-2004: Analysis of Panel Data", Working Paper No.384, Centre for Development Studies, Thiruvananthapuram.

Zachariah, M. and Sooryamoorthy, R. (1994), "Science for Social Revolution: Achievements and Dilemmas of a Development Movement", The Kerala Sastra Sahitya Parishad, London: Zed Books.

Bibliography

Bibliography

Aakel K.V. and Kidambi, Soumya (2007), "Challenging Corruption with Social Audit", *Economic and Political Weekly,* February 3.

Acharya, Meena and Lynn Bennett (1983), "Women and the Subsistence Sector: Economic Participation and Household Decision Making in Nepal", World Bank Staff Working Papers, No. 526, The World Bank, Washington, D.C.

Adhikari, A. and Bhatia, K. (2010), "NREGA Wage Payments: Can We Bank on the Banks?" *Economic and Political Weekly*, January 2.

Ahluwalia, I.J. (1991), "Productivity and Growth in Indian Manufacturing", Oxford University Press, Oxford.

Ahluwalia, Montek (2000), "Economic Performance of States in Post Reforms Period", *Economic and Political Weekly*, May 4.

Ahuja, U.R. et al. (2011), "Impact of MGNREGA on Rural Employment and Migration: A Study in Agriculturally-Backward and Agriculturally-Advanced Districts of Haryana", *Agricultural Economics Research Review.*

Akhtar, S.M. Jawed and Azeez, N.P. Abdul (2011), "MGNREGS: Employer of Last Resort: A Special Reference to Kerala", published in *Indian Economic Journal*, Challenges of Inclusive Growth, Special Issue, December.

Akhtar, S.M. Jawed and Azeez, N.P. Abdul (2012), "NREGA and Poverty Reduction in India", published in Bhabesh Sen and Mitali Chinara (eds.), *Economic Development and Poverty in India*, New Century Publications, New Delhi.

Akhtar, S.M. Jawed and Azeez, N.P. Abdul (2012), "MGNREGS: A Tool for Sustainable Environment", published in *Kurukshetra*, Volume 60, No. 8, April.

Akhtar, S.M. Jawed and Azeez, N.P. Abdul (2012), "Budgetary Allocation and its Utilization under MGNREGS: An Overview", published in *Kurukshetra*, Volume 60, No. 6, April.

Akhtar, S.M. Jawed and Azeez, N.P. Abdul (2012), "Rural Employment Guarantee Programme and Migration", published in *Kurukshetra*, Volume 60, No. 4, February.

Akhtar, S.M. Jawed, Azeez, N.P. Abdul and Alam, Md. Masroor (2012), "Rural Women Empowerment through MGNREGS in the State of Kerala", published in A.K. Thakur and S.M. Jawed Akhtar (eds.), *Non-Farm Sector and Rural Transformation*, Deep & Deep Publications Pvt. Ltd., New Delhi.

Akhtar, S.M. Jawed, Azeez, N.P. Abdul and Alam, Md. Masroor (2011), "Towards Millennium Development Goals and the Role of MGNREGA", published in *Kurukshetra*, Volume 60, No. 2, December.

Ambasta, P., Shankar, P.S.V. and Shah, M. (2008), "Two Years of NREGA: The Road Ahead", *Economic and Political Weekly*, February, 23.

Anand, S. (2002), "Self Help Groups in Empowering Women: Case Study of Selected SHGs and NHGs", Discussion Paper 38, Kerala Research Programme on Local Level Development, *Centre for Development Studies*, Thiruvanathapuram.

Anitha, S., Reshma, B., Devika, J., Ranjini, K., Nisha, P.S. and Kodoth, P. (2008), "Gendering Governance or Governing Women? Politics, Patriarchy and Democratic Decentralization in Kerala State, India", *Centre for Development Studies*, Thiruvanathapuram.

Antonopoulos, R. (2009), "Promoting Gender Equality through Stimulus Packages and Public Job Creation: Lessons Learned from South Africa's Expanded Public Works Programme", Public Policy Brief, No. 101, Annandale-on-Hudson, NY, The Levy Economics Institute of Bard College.

Apte, M.D. (1975), "Education and Unemployment in Kerala", *Economic and Political Weekly*, 12th July.

Arnab, K. Basu, Chau, Nancy H. and Kanbur, Ravi (2008), "A Theory of Employment Guarantees: Contestability, Creditability and Distributional Concerns", www.elsevier.com/ locate/econbase or www.sciense direct.com.

Arun, T. and Mosley, P. (2003), "Improving Access to Rural Finance in India: Supply Side Constraints", Background Paper to the Economic and Sector Work Study on Access to Finance, Washington, D.C.: South Asia Finance and Private Sector Development Unit, World Bank.

Arun, J. and Varghese, R. (2006), "Reasonable Beginning in Palakkad, Kerala", *Economic and Political Weekly*, Volume 41, No. 48, December 2-8.

Azeez, N.P. Abdul and Akhtar, S.M. Jawed (2013), "Relevance of Keynesian Macro Economic Theories in Policy Making-A Case

Study of MGNREGA in India", published in *Prajanan, Journal of Social & Management Science*, NIBM, Volume XLII, No. 1, Pune, April-June.

Azeez, N.P. Abdul and Akthar, S.M. Jawed (2012), *Economy of Kerala: A Development Experience*, Lambert Academic Publishing, Germany.

Azeez, N.P. Abdul and Akhtar, S.M. Jawed (2011), "Financial Inclusion through MGNREGS: A Special Reference to Kerala", published in *International Journal of Micro Finance*, Volume 1, No. 2, Pondicherry, July-December.

Azeez, N.P. Abdul and Akhtar, S.M. Jawed (2012), "Women Empowerment in India: A Study Based on Index of Women Empowerment in India", published in *International Journal of Research in Commerce, Economics and Management*, Volume 2, No. 5, Haryana, May.

Bablu, J.S. (2002), "Parties, Communal Bodies' Hijack, SHG Concept", *The Hindu*.

Banerjee, A.V. (2008), "Why Fighting Poverty is Hard?", Unpublished, MIT (mimeo).

Banerjee, K. and Saha, P. (2010), "The NREGA: The Maoists and the Development Woes of Indian State", *Economic and Political Weekly*, July 5.

Balan, P.P. and Retna, Raj M. (2006), "Decentralized Governance and Poverty Reduction: Lessons from Kerala", Kerala Institute of Local Administration, Thrissur.

Barrett, C., Holden, S. and Clay, D.C. (2004), "Can Food for Work Programmes Reduce Vulnerability?" in S. Dercon (ed.), Insurance Against Poverty, Oxford University Press, Oxford.

Banerjee, K. and Saha, P. (2010), "The NREGA, The Maoists and The Development Woes of Indian State", *Economic and Political Weekly*, December 4.

Basu, K. (1981), "Food for Work Programmes: Beyond Roads That Get Washed Away", *Economic and Political Weekly,* June 5.

Basu, Arnab K., Chau, Nancy H. and Kanbur, Ravi (2005), "The National Rural Employment Guarantee Act of India, 2005", Department of Applied Economics and Management, Cornell University, Ithaca, NY.

Basu, Alaka Malwade (1996), "Women's Economic Roles and Child Health: An Overview", in *Population and Women,* New York, Population Division, UN.

Basu, A., Chau, N. and Kanbur, R. (2007), *The National Rural Employment Guarantee Act of India*, 2005, Mimeo.

Basu, A.K. (2011), "Impact Of Rural Employment Guarantee Schemes on Seasonal Labour Markets: Optimum Compensation and Workers' Welfare", *IZA* Discussion Paper No. 5701, College of William and Mary, ZEF, University of Bonn and IZA.

Bhattacharya, R. and Sudarshan, R.M. (2008), "NREGA in Abu Road: Rajasthan", paper presented at Employment Opportunities and Public Employment Policy in Globalizing India, 3-5 April, Centre for Development Studies, Thiruvananthapuram.

Bhatty, Kiran (2006), "Employment Guarantee and Child Rights", *Economic and Political Weekly*, 20th May.

Behera, B. (2006), "Determinants of Sustainable Management of Natural Resources: The Case of Joint Forest Management in India", *Cuvillier Verlag GÖttingen*, Germany.

Bhatia, B. and Dreze, J. (2006), "Employment Guarantee in Jharkhand: Ground Realities", *Economic and Political Weekly*, July 22.

Bisht, Arvind Singh (2006), "Rural Employment: No Guarantee Yet", *The Times of India*, New Delhi, 19th February.

Blumberg, Rae Lesser (1991), (ed.), "Gender, Family and Economy: The Triple Overlap", Sage Publications, U.S.A.

Brahmananda, P.R. and Panchamukhi, V.R. (ed.), "The Development Process of the Indian Economy", Himalaya Publishing Company, Delhi.

Bruce, Judith and Dwyer, Daisy (1988), "Introduction', in Daisy Dwyer and Judith Bruce" (eds.), "A Home Divided: Women and Income in the Third World", Stanford University Press, Stanford.

Burra, Ranadive and Murthy (2005), "Micro-Credit, Poverty and Empowerment: Linking the Triad", Sage Publications, New Delhi.

Cain, Glen (1966), "Married Women in the Labour Force: An Economic Analysis", The University of Chicago Press, Chicago.

CESS (2009), "NREGS in Andhra Pradesh: Issues and Challenges", Centre for Economic and Social Studies, Hyderabad.

Centre for Development Studies (1975), "Poverty, Unemployment and Development Policy: A Case Study of Selected Review with Reference to Kerala", UN Publication, New York.

Centre for Development Support (2006), "First Monitoring Report, Prepared by Samarthan with Support from Poorest Area Civil Society Programme (PACS)", Status of NREGA Implementation: Grassroots Learning and Way Forward.

Centre for Science and Environment (undated), "An Ecological Act: A Backgrounder to the National Rural Employment Guarantee Act (NREGA)", Draft, Prepared by Natural Resource Management and Livelihood Unit, New Delhi.

Chakraborty, Pinaki, (2007), "Implementation of Employment Guarantee: A Preliminary Appraisal", *Economic and Political Weekly*, Volume 42 (7).

Chakravarti, Sauvik (2006), "Employment Guarantee a Hoax", *Indian Express*, New Delhi, 6th August.

Chandrasekhar, C.P., and Ghosh, J. (2005), "Social Inclusion in the NREGS", *Business Line* (India), January 27.

Chandrashekar, C.P. and Ghosh, J. (2009), "Bid to Boost Women's Share in NREGS", *The Hindu Business Line*, January 12.

Chathukulam, Jos and Gireesan, K. (2007), "Employment to the Tribal Communities under NREGS: A Case from Wayanad, Kerala", Monitoring Report.

Chathukulam, Jos and Gireesan, K. (2007): "Impact Assessment of NREGS in Kerala: Evaluation of Systems and Processes", Centre for Rural Management, Kottayam, Kerala. Report Submitted to Ministry of Rural Development, Government of India, New Delhi.

Chathukulam, Jos and Gireesan, K. (2010), "Employment to the Tribal Communities under NREGS: A Case from Wayanad, Kerala", Monitoring Report

Chathukulam, J. and John, M.S. (2002), "Five Years of Participatory Planning in Kerala, Rhetoric and Reality", Economic and Political Weekly, Volume 37 (49).

Chavan P., Ram, R.K. (2002), "Micro Credit and Rural Poverty: An Analysis of Empirical Evidence", *Economic and Political Weekly*, March 9, No. 10.

Chavan, P. and Bedamatta, R. (2006), "Trends in Agricultural Wages in India: 1964-65 to 1999-2000", in *Economic and Political Weekly*, Volume 41, No. 38, 23-29 September.

Cherunilam, Francis (1995), "Kerala Economy: Problems and Prospects", in P.J. Gandhi (ed.) Indian Economic Issues (part II) Jaipur: Pointer Publishers.

Chhabra, Sangeeta, Raina, R.L. and Sharma, G.L. (2009), "A Report on Management of National Rural Employment Guarantee Scheme: Issues and Challenges", Lal Bahadur Shastri Institute of Management, Delhi.

Comptroller Auditor General of India (2007), Performance Audit of Implementation of National Rural Employment Guarantee Act, 2005 (NREGA).

CRM, CSES and SDC-Capdeck (2003), "Emerging Issues in Panchayati Raj in Kerala: A Study Report, Thiruvananthapuram.

Dasgupta, Swapan (2005), "Rename REGA as Corruption Guarantee Scheme", *The Pioneer*, New Delhi, 14th August.

Datt, R. (2008), "Dismal Experience of NREGA: Lessons for the Future", *Mainstream*, Volume 46, No. 17, 12th April.

Dey, Subhasish and Bedi, Arjun S. (2010), "The National Rural Employment Guarantee Scheme in Birbhum District", *Economic and Political Weekly*, October 9.

Dev, S. Mahendra (1995), "India's (Maharashtra) Employment Guarantee Scheme: Lessons from Long Experience", in J. Von Braun (ed.), Employment for Poverty Reduction and Food Security, International Food Policy Research Institute, Washington D.C.

Dey, S., Ravi, C., Viswanathan, B., Gulati, A. and Ramachandar, S. (2004), "Economic Liberalization, Targeted Programmes and Household Food Security: A Case Study of India", Discussion Paper No. 68, Markets, Trade and Industry Division, International Food Policy Research Institute, Washington D.C.

Devi, L. (2001), "Education, Employment and Job Preference of Women in Kerala: A Micro-Level Case Study", Discussion Paper No. 42, KRPLLD.

Deolalikar, A.B. (1995), "Special Employment Programme and Poverty Alleviation", *Asian Development Review,* Volume 13, No. 2.

—(1990), "Famine Prevention in India", in J. Dreze and A.K. Sen (eds.), The Political Economy of Hunger, Clarendon, Oxford.

Desai, Sonalde and Jain, D. (1994), "Maternal Employment and Changes in the Family Dynamics: The Social Context of Women's Work in Rural South India", *Population and Development Review,* Volume 20, No. 1.

Devereux, S. and Solomon, C. (2006), "Employment Creation Programmes: The International Experience, Issues in

Employment and Poverty", Discussion Paper 24, Geneva, ILO.

Devika, J. (2007), "Fears of Contagion? De-Politicization and Recent Conflicts over Politics in Kerala", *Economic and Political Weekly*, June 23.

Devika, J., and Thampy, B. (2007), "Between 'Empowerment' and 'Liberation': The Kudumbashree Initiative in Kerala", *Indian Journal of Gender Studies*, 14(1).

Dixon, Ruth (1978), "Counting Women in Agricultural Labour Force", *Population and Development Review*, Volume 8, No. 3.

Dreze, Jean (2006), "National Employment Guarantee Inaction", *The Hindu*, Chennai, 12th September.

—(2007), "NREGA: Dismantling the Contractor Raj", *The Hindu*, 20th November.

Dreze, Jean, Khera, R. and Siddharth (2007), "NREGA in Orissa: Ten Loopholes and the Silver Lining; Interim Survey Report" (Mimeo), Survey Conducted by G.B Pant Science Institute.

Dreze, Jean and Oldiges, Christian (2007), "Commendable Act", *Frontline*, Volume 24, Issue 14, July.

Dreze, Jean, Dev, N. and Khera, R. (2006), "Employment Guarantee: A Primer", New Delhi, NBT.

Dreze, Jean, Khera, R. and Siddharth (2008), "Corruption in NREGA: Myths and Reality", *The Hindu,* January 22.

Dreze, Jean and Khera, R. (2009), "The Battle for Employment Guarantee", *Frontline*, Volume 26, No. 1, January.

Dreze, Jean, and Oldiges, C. (2009), "Livelihood Issues", *Frontline*, Volume 26, No. 4, February.

Dreze, Jean and Khera, R. (2009), "Battle for Work", *Frontline,* Volume 26, No. 1, January.

Dreze, Jean and Oldiges, C. (2009), "Work in Progress", *Frontline*, Volume 26, Issue IV, February.

Dreze, Jean and Sen, A. (1989), "Hunger and Public Action", Oxford University Press, Oxford and Delhi.

Dreze, Jean and Sen, A. (1996), "Indian Development: Selected Regional Perspectives", New Delhi: Oxford University Press.

Eapen, Mrldul (1974), "Some Aspects of Unemployment Problem in Kerala", CDS Working Paper No. 74.

Eapen, M. (1994), The Changing Structure of the Workforce in Kerala, in B.A. Prakash (ed.) Kerala's Economy: Performance, Problems, and Prospects, New Delhi: Sage.

Folbre, Nancy, Bergman, B., Agarwal, Bina and Floro, M. (eds.)

(1991), "Women's Work in the World Economy", Macmillan, London.

Gaiha, Raghav, (2005), "Does the Employment Guarantee Scheme Benefit the Rural Poor in India, Some Recent Evidence", *Asian Survey*, Volume 45, No. 6, November-December.

Gaiha, R. and Imai, K. (2006), "The Maharashtra Employment Guarantee Scheme-India", Briefing Paper; Overseas Development Institute (ODI), Inter-Regional Inequality Facility, Policy Brief, February 6.

Ganesh Kumar, A., Mishra, S. and Panda, M. (2004), "Employment Guarantee for Rural India", *Economic and Political Weekly,* December 18.

Gopalan, S., Bhupathy, R. and Raja, H. (1995), "Appraisal of Success Factors in Nutrition Relevant Programs: A Case Study of Alappuzha Community Based Nutrition Programme", Chennai: United Nations Children's Fund.

Government of India (2002), "National Human Development Report, 2001", Planning Commission, Oxford University Press, New Delhi.

——(2005), Infant Mortality Rate, 2005, Office of the Registrar General of India, Ministry of Home Affairs, New Delhi, (2009), Extracts from Official Reports.

——(2008), "Kerala Development Report", Planning Commission, New Delhi, Academic Foundation, India.

Government of Kerala, (1996), "Report of the First State Finance Commission", Government of Kerala, Trivandrum.

——(2001), "Report of the Second State Finance Commission", Government of Kerala, Trivandrum.

——(2005), "Report of the Third State Finance Commission", Government of Kerala, Trivandrum.

——(2008), "Report of the Kerala Public Expenditure Review Committee", November, Kerala, Trivandrum.

Greene, W.H. (2003), "Econometric Analysis", Pearson Education Pvt. Ltd., Delhi, India.

Gujarati, D.N. and Sangeetha (2007), "Basic Econometrics", Tata McGraw Hill, New Delhi.

Heller, P. (2001), "Moving the State: The Politics of Democratic Decentralization in Kerala", South Africa, and Porto Alegre, *Politics and Society*, 29(1).

Heller, P., Harilal, K.N., and Chaudhari, S. (2007), "Building Local

Democracy: Evaluating the Impact of Decentralization in Kerala", India, *World Development*, 35(4).

Hirway, Indira (1986), "Wage Employment Programmes in Rural Development", Oxford and Publishing House, New Delhi.

Hirway, I. (2004), "Providing Employment Guarantee in India: Some Critical Issues", *Economic and Political Weekly*, Volume 39, No. 48, 27 November-3 December.

Hirway, I. (2005), "Enhancing Livelihood Security through the National Employment Guarantee Act: Towards Effective Operationalization of the Act, *Indian Journal of Labour Economics*, Volume 48, November 4, Centre for Development Alternatives Ahmedabad.

Institute of Social Studies Trust (2006), "Study on Women and NREGA", Mimeo, New Delhi: ILO and ISST.

Institute of Social Studies Trust (2007), "Women and NREGA", Mimeo, New Delhi: ILO and ISST.

Institute of Social Studies Trust (2009),"Examining the NREGA: Women's Participation and Impacts", Paper Presented in National Workshop on National Rural Employment Guarantee in India: Lessons from Implementation, Bangalore 8-9 September, Organized by the Institute for Human Development and the ISST, New Delhi.

Isaac, T.M. and Franke, Richard W. (2000), "Local Democracy and Development", New Delhi: Left Word.

Isaac, T.M. (2000), "Campaign for Democratic Decentralization in Kerala: An Assessment from the Perspective of Empowered Deliberative Democracy", Mimeo.

——(2001), Campaign for Democratic Decentralization in Kerala, *Social Scientist*.

Isaac, T.M. (2004), "Democratic Decentralization and Women Empowerment: Kerala Model", Paper Presented at International Expert Group Meeting on Local Level Gender Responsive Budgeting, NIPFP, New Delhi.

Isaac, T.Mm and Tharakan, M.P.K. (2004), "Kerala: Towards a New Agenda", *Economic and Political Weekly*, Volume 30, No. 31/32, August.

Isaac, T.M. and Heller, Peter (2002), "Decentralization, Democracy and Development: People's Campaign for Decentralized Planning in Kerala", in A. Fung and E.O. Wright (eds.), Deepening Democracy: Institutional Innovations in Empowered

Participatory Democracy, London: Verso Press.

Isaac, T.M., Williams, P.C. and Thampi, B.V. (2002), "Women Neighbourhood Groups: Towards a New Perspective, Paper Presented at the Seminar on Decentralization, Sustainable Development and Social Security Kudumbashree.

Iqbal, Mohammad (2006), "Public Vigilance Helps to Minimize Corruption in Rural Employment Guarantee Scheme", *The Hindu*, 28th April.

Jacob, A. and Varghese, R. (2006), "NREGA Implementation-I: Reasonable Beginning in Palakkad Kerala", *Economic and Political Weekly*, Volume 41, No. 48, 2-8 December.

Jain, Devaki (1979), "Impact on Women Workers: Maharashtra Employment Guarantee Scheme", Mimeo, New Delhi: ISST.

Jha, R., Bhattacharya, S., Gaiha, R. and Shankar, S. (2009), "Capture of Anti-Poverty Programs: An Analysis of the National Rural Employment Guarantee Program in India", *Journal of Asian Economics*, 20(4).

Jha, R., Gaiha, R. and Shankar, S. (2008), "Reviewing the National Rural Employment Guarantee Programme", *Economic and Political Weekly*, 43(10).

Jha, R., Gaiha, R. and Shankar, S. (2009), "National Rural Employment Guarantee Programme in Andhra Pradesh", *Economic and Political Weekly*, Volume 53, No. 48, 2-8 December.

Jha, R., Gaiha, R. and Pandey, M.K. (2010), "Determinants of Employment in India's National Rural Employment Guarantee Scheme", ASARC Working Paper 17, Australia South Asia Research Centre, The Australian National University, Canberra, Australia.

John, J. (2009), "A Study on Kudumbashree Project: A Poverty Eradication Programme in Kerala, Performance, Impact and Lessons for Other States", New Delhi, Kerala Development Society.

Johnson, D. and Tannirkulam, A. (2009), "NREGA in Andhra Pradesh: Seven Lessons from the Data", CMF Focus Note No. 4, Chennai, Centre for Micro Finance, November.

Jose, T.K. (2006), "Kudumbashree: Urban CDS, A Community Based Women Oriented Initiative to Fight Urban Poverty in Kerala", *Productivity News*, National Productivity Council, New Delhi, Volume 44, No. 2, March-April.

Joshi, Anuradha (2009), "Do Right Work? Law, Activism, and the Employment Guarantee Scheme", www.elsevier.com/ locate/econbase or www.sciencedirect.com.

Joshi, Varsha, Singh, S. and Joshi, K.N. (2008), "Evaluation of NREGS in Rajasthan", Institute of Development Studies, Jaipur.

Kabeer, Naila (2010), "Gender and Social Protection Strategies in the Informal Economy", New Delhi: Routledge.

Kadiyala, S. (2004), "Scaling up Kudumbashree-Collective Action for Poverty Alleviation and Women's Empowerment", FCND Discussion Paper 180, Washington, D.C.: International Food Policy Research Institute.

Kanchi, A. (2009), "Women in Agriculture", Presented at Conference on Women's Employment in India, New Delhi, ILO.

Kannan, K.P. (1983), "Cashew Development in India: Potentialities and Constraint", Agricole Publishing Company, New Delhi.

Kannan, K.P., Thempakkan, K.R., Ramankutty, V, and Aravindan, K.P. (1991), "Health and Development in Rural Kerala", Kerala Sahitya Parishad, Trivandrum.

Kannan, K.P. (2005), "Kerala's Turnaround in Growth: Role of Social Development, Remittances and Reform", *Economic and Political Weekly*, Volume 40, No. 6, February 4.

Karat, Brinda (2004), "No Jobs Ahead: Dilution in Employment Guarantee", www.timesofindia.indiatimes.com, 10th December.

Karat, Brinda (2005), "Towards Implementing the Rural Employment Guarantee Act", *People's Democracy*, October 24.

Khera, R. (2008), "Empowerment Guarantee Act", *Economic and Political Weekly*, Volume 43, No. 35, 30 August-5 September.

Khera, Nayak N. (2009), "Women Workers and Perceptions of the National Rural Employment Guarantee Act", *Economic and Political Weekly*, Volume 44, No. 43, 24-30 October.

Kishore, Sunita (1996), "Urban Women's Employment Trajectories in Ghana and Bolivia", Occasional Papers, No. 5, Macro InternationalInc, Calverton, Maryland.

Kumbhar, S. (2009), "Has the Congress Earned Dividend from NREGA?," *Mainstream Weekly*, Volume XLVII, No. 23, 23rd May, http://knowledge.nrega.net/985.

Kodoth, P. and Eapen, M. (2005), "Looking Beyond Gender Parity Gender Inequities of Some Dimensions of Well-being in

Kerala", *Economic and Political Weekly*, July 23.

Krishna, Anirudh (2001), "Moving from the Stock of Social Capital to the Flow of Benefits: The Role of Agency", *World Development*, Volume 29, No. 6.

—(2006), "Poverty and Democratic Participation Reconsidered: Evidence from the Local Level in India", *Comparative Politics*, Volume 38, No. 4.

Local Self Government Department (2006), "National Rural Employment Guarantee Act, 2005", Government of Kerala, Trivandrum.

Mannathukkaren, N. (2010), "The 'Poverty' of Political Society: Partha Chatterjee and the People's Plan Campaign in Kerala", *Third World Quarterly*, 31(2).

Mansuri, G. and Rao, V. (2004), "Community-Based and Driven Development: A Critical Review, World Bank Policy Research Working Paper 3209, Washington, D.C.: The World Bank.

Mathew, E.T. (1997), "Employment and Unemployment in Kerala, Some Neglected Aspects", Sage Publications, New Delhi.

—(1991), "Financing Higher Education: Sources and Uses of Funds of Private Colleges in Kerala", New Delhi.

—(1995), "Educated Unemployment in Kerala: Some Socio-Economic Aspects", *Economic and Political Weekly*, 30(6), February 11.

Mehrotra, S. (2008), "NREGA, Two Years On: Where Do We Go from Here?", *Economic and Political Weekly*, Volume 43, No. 31, August 8.

Mehta, A.K. and Shah, A. (2003), "Chronic Poverty in India: Incidence, Causes and Policies", *World Development*, Volume 31, No. 3, March.

Ministry of Rural Development (2009), MoRD (2005a), "The National Rural Employment Guarantee Act 2005 (NREGA): Operational Guidelines (1st Edition)", Ministry of Rural Development, Government of India, New Delhi.

—(2005b), "MIS for National Rural Employment Guarantee Act 2005: A User Manual", Ministry of Rural Development, Government of India, New Delhi.

—(2008), "The National Rural Employment Guarantee Act, 2005 (NREGA): Operational Guidelines (3rd edition)", Ministry of Rural Development, Government of India, New Delhi.

—(2009), "A Study on the Performance of NREGS in Kerala",

UNDP, New Delhi.
—(2009), Minutes of Meeting on 'Policy for Revising Wage Rate Fixed under Section 6(1) of NREGA', Held on 10th July, in the Chamber of Secretary Rural Development, Krishi Bhavan, New Delhi, http://nrega.nic.in/circular/Minutes_meeting10july09.pdf.

Moore, M. and Jadhav, V. (2006), "The Politics and Bureaucratic of Rural Public Works: Maharashtra's Employment Guarantee Scheme", *Journal of Development Studies*, Volume 42, No. 8.

Mukherjee, Chandan and Issac, T.M.T. (1991), "Study of Educated Unemployed in Kerala: Report of the Sample Survey of Registrants of Employment Exchange", Centre for Development Studies, Kerala (mimeograph).

Mukherjee, C. and Issac, T.M.T (1994), "A Review of the Self-Employment Programmes for Educated Unemployment in Kerala: Some Neglected Aspects", Sage Publications, New Delhi.

Mukhopadhyay, S. (2007), "The Enigma of the Kerala Woman: A Failed Promise of Literacy", New Delhi: Social Science Press.

Murgai, R. and Ravallion, M. (2005), "Employment Guarantee in Rural India: What would it Cost and How Much will it Reduce Poverty", *Economic and Political Weekly*, 40(31), August 4.

Nagaraj, K. (1999), "Labour Market Characteristics and Employment Generation Programmes in India" in Barbara Harriss-White and S. Subramanian (eds.), Ill-fare in India, Sage Publications, New Delhi.

Nair, G. (2000), "People's Planning: The Kerala Experience", Discussion Paper No. 16, Kerala Research Programme on Local Level Development, CDS, Kerala.

Narayanan, Sudha (2008), "Employment Guarantee, Women's Work and Childcare", *Economic and Political Weekly*, March 1.

National Council of Applied Economic Research (2008), "Study on Perception of Disadvantaged in Seven States of India", Draft Report, Volume I and II, New Delhi.

—(2009), NCAER-PIF Study on Evaluating Performance of National Rural Employment Guarantee Act, New Delhi.

National Rural Employment Guarantee Scheme (NREGS) (2005), Gazette Notification, Government of India.

Nayak, S. (2010), "Participation of Rural Poor in Mahatma Gandhi NREGP: A Comparative Study of Mayurbhanj and Balasore

Districts of Orissa", Dissertation (unpublished), North Orissa University.

——(2012), "Participation in a Rural Employment Guarantee Programme: Evidence from India", LAP Lambert Academic Publishing, Saarbrücken, Germany.

NCAER-PIF (2009), "Study on Evaluating Performance of National Rural Employment Guarantee Act", NCAER, New Delhi.

NREGS Handbook for Local Self Governments (2008), Kerala Institute of Local Administration (KILA), Mulamkunnathukavu, Thrissur.

NSSO (2006), "Employment and Unemployment in India, 2004-05", Report 515(1), MOSPI, Government of India.

NSSO (2006), "Nutritional Intake in India, 2004-05", Report 513, MOSPI, Government of India, Palmer.

Oommen, M.A. (1993), Essays on Kerala Economy, New Delhi: Oxford University Press.

——(1999), "The Community Development Society of Kerala", Institute of Social Sciences, New Delhi.

——(2000), "Dreze-Sen Theory of Public Action and Kerala's Development Experience", Institute of Social Sciences, New Delhi.

——(2008), Micro Financing Institutions in Kerala and Grameen Bank: A Comparative Study, in Micro Finance: Non-Micro Potentials and Problems (Malayalam), Eqbal. B. (ed.).

——(2009), "Microfinance and Poverty Alleviation: The Case of Kerala's Kudumbashree", Working Paper 17, Kochi, Kerala: Centre for Socio-Economic and Environmental Studies.

Oommen, M.A. and Ghosh (2005), "Decentralization and Poverty Reduction: A Case Study of Kerala and West Bengal", A UNDP Sponsored Unpublished Study, Institute of Social Sciences, New Delhi.

Osella, Filippo and Osella, Caroline (2000), "Social Mobility in Kerala: Modernity and Identity in Conflict", Pluto, London.

Palriwala, R. and Neetha, N. (2009), "The Care Diamond: State Social Policy and the Market", Research Report 3, India, UNRISD Project on Political and Social Economy of Care.

Panda, B. (2000), "Rural-Non Farm Employment in India's North-East: Facts, Significance and Policy Implications", *Journal of NEICSSR,* Volume 24, No. 1, Shillong, India.

Pankaj, A. and Sharma, A. (2006), "Evaluation and Impact

Assessment of National Rural Employment Guarantee Act in Bihar", Institute for Human Development, New Delhi.

Pankaj, A. (2008), "Processes, Institutions, and Mechanisms of Implementation of NREGA: Impact Assessment of Bihar and Jharkhand", Sponsored by Ministry of Rural Development, GoI and UNDP, Institute for Human Development, New Delhi.

Pankaj, A. and Tankha, R. (2009), "Women's Empowerment through Guaranteed Employment: A Case Study of NREGA Implementation in Bihar, Jharkhand, Rajasthan, and Himachal Pradesh, Sponsored by UNIFEM, Institute for Human Development, New Delhi.

Pankaj, A. and Tankha, R. (2010), "Empowerment Effects of the NREGS on Women Workers: A Study in Four States", *Economic and Political Weekly*, Volume 45, No. 30, 24-30 July.

Papadimitriou, D.B. (2008), Promoting Equality through an Employment of Last Resort Policy, Working Paper No. 545, October, Annandale-on-Hudson, NY, The Levy Economics Institute of Bard College.

Parikh, K., Deve, M. and Shariff, A. (2007), "Anti-Poverty Programs in India: Are they Pro-Poor?", in A. Gulati and S. Fan (eds.) The Dragon and the Elephant: Agricultural and Rural Reforms in Chinaand India, New Delhi: Oxford University Press.

Patnaik, Prabhat (2005), "On the Need for Providing Employment Guarantee", *Economic and Political Weekly*, January 15.

Pinstrup, Andersen P. (1993) (ed.), The Political Economy of Food and Nutrition Policies, Johns Hopkins University Press, Baltimore, Md., USA.

Placid, G. (2009), "National Rural Employment Guarantee Scheme (NREGS): Perspectives and Implementation Mechanism in Kerala", *Catalyst*, Newsletter of Cyriac Elias Voluntary Association (CEVA), Kochi, Volume VII, Issue 2.

Prakash, B.A. (1988), "Unemployment in Kerala", CDS Working Paper No. 230, Thiruvananthapuram.

Prakash, B.A. (1988), Changing Structure of Employment in Kerala, Margin, October-December.

Prakash, B.A. (ed.) (1999), "Kerala's Economic Development: Performance and Problems in the Post-liberalization Period", Sage Publications, New Delhi.

PRIA (2006), "National Consultation on Implementation of NREGA: Experiences and Ways Forward", 1st June.

Psacharopoulos, G. and Tzannatos, Z. (1991), "Female Labour Force Participation and Education", in G. Psacharopoulos (ed.) Essays on Poverty, Equity and Growth, Pergamon Press for the World Bank, Oxford.

Radhakrishnan, R. (2009), "National Rural Employment Guarantee Programme in Kerala", *Sasthragathi*, February.

Rajsekhar, B. (2009), "Transparency and Accountability Initiatives: The Social Audit Experience in Andhra Pradesh", Workshop on National Rural Employment Guarantee in India-Lessons from Implementation, Institute for Human Development and Institute of Social Studies Trust, Bangalore.

Rao, M. Govinda, Chakraborty, Lekha and Bagchi, Amaresh (2006), "Fiscal Decentralization and Local Level Gender Responsive Budgeting: An Empirical Analysis of Five Countries", NIPFP mimeo, New Delhi.

Rao, M. Govinda (ed.) (2002), "Development, Poverty, and Fiscal Policy", New Delhi: Oxford University Press.

Rao, M. Govinda and Nirvikar Singh, (2004), "Asymmetric Federalism in India", National Institute of Public Finance and Policy, Working Paper 6, New Delhi.

Ratna and Sudarn (2008), "Examining the NREGA: Women's Participation and Impacts", Institute of Social Studies Trust, New Delhi.

Reddy, D.N. et al. (2010), "National Rural Employment Guarantee as Social Protection", in *IDS Bulletin*, Volume 41, No. 4, July.

Roy, A. and Dey, N. (2009), "NREGA Breaking the Feudally Enforced Silence", One World South Asia, 9th July.

Sainath, P. (2007), "Employment Guarantee: No Place for Single Women", *India Together*, 20th July 2007, www.indiatogether.org/2007/may/psa-nregs.htm.

Sarkar, S. (2008), "Trends and Patterns of Labour Supply and Unemployment in India", ILO Asia-Pacific Working Paper Series, New Delhi, ILO.

Scandizzo, P., Gaiha, R., and Imai, K. (2007), "Does the Employment Guarantee Scheme Stabilize the Incomes of Households in Rural India?'; Paper Provided by Economics, University of Manchester, The School of Economics Discussion Paper Series, Number 6.

Sen, A. (1981), "Poverty and Famine: An Essay on Entitlement and Deprivation", Oxford University Press, New York.

——(1986), "Food, Economics and Entailments", *Lloyds Bank Review*, Volume 160.

Shah, A., Mehta, A.K. and Bhide, S. (2006), "Chronic Poverty in India: Evidence and Policy Imperatives", New Delhi, NCAER.

Shah, Mihir (2004), "National Rural Employment Guarantee Act: A Historic Opportunity", *Economic and Political Weekly*, December 8.

Shah, Mihir (2009b), "Multiplier Accelerator Synergy in NREGA", *The Hindu,* 30th April.

——(2009c), "Taking Goals of NREGA-I Forward", *The Hindu*, 14th August.

Shah, Deepak and Sovan Mohanty (2010), "Implementation of NREGA during Eleventh Plan in Maharashtra", *Indian Journal of Agricultural Economics*,Volume 65, No. 3.

Shariff, Abusaleh (2007), "How to Find the Poor", Editorial Article, *Times of India*, August 10, New Delhi.

——(2008), "Access and Use of India's National Rural Employment Guarantee Scheme: An Empirical Assessment", Mimeo, IFPRI, New Delhi.

——(2009), "Assessment of Outreach and Benefits of National Rural Employment Guarantee Scheme of India", *The Indian Journal of Labour Economics*, Volume 52, No. 2.

Sharma, R. (2003), "Kerala's Decentralization: Idea in Practice', *Economic and Political Weekly*, September 6.

Streeten, Paul (2002), "Empowerment, Participation and the Poor", Occasional Paper, Human Development Report Office, United Nations Development Programme, New York.

Sridhar, V. (2005), "Empowering the Rural Poor", *Frontline*, Volume 22, Issue 19, September 10-23.

Srikumar, C., Krishna, P.K. and Rajalakshmi K. (2008), "Panchayat Resource Mapping to Panchayat-Level Planning in Kerala: An Analytical Study".

Srinivasan, T.N. (2000), "Eight Lectures on India's Economic Reforms", Oxford University Press, New Delhi.

Srivastava, V. (2000), "The Impact of India's Economic Reforms on Industrial Productivity, Efficiency and Competitiveness", Report of a Project Sponsored by the Industrial Development Bank of India, National Council of Applied Economic Research (NCAER), New Delhi.

Sudarshan, M. Ratna (2009), "NREGA in Palakkad, Kerala",

Presented at IHD-UNIFEM Workshop, Women's Employment through Guaranteed Employment", 31st August, 2009, IIC, New Delhi.

Sudarshan, M. Ratna (2010), "Women's Participation in the NREGA: The Interplay between Wage Work and Care", Chronic Poverty Research Centre, Draft, June.

Sudarshan, R.M. and Bhattacharya, S. (2008), "Through the Magnifying Glass: Women's Work and Labour Force Participation in Urban Delhi", ILO Asia-Pacific Working Paper Series, May.

Tanzi, V. (2000), "Corruption, Governmental Activities, and Markets", in V. Tanzi, Policies, Institutions and the Dark Side of Economics, Cheltenham: Edward Elgar.

UNDP (2006), Sponsored Solution Exchange for Decentralization Community: Summary of Discussion on Query: Self-help Groups and PRIs, posted on 18th January, www.solutionexchange-un.net.in.

UNDP (2009), Sponsored Solution Exchange for Decentralization Community: Summary of discussion on Query: Self-help Groups as Anti-Poverty Vehicles in Panchayati Raj Experiences, posted on 26th February, www.solutionexchange-un.net.in.

United Nations Development Programme (UNDP) (2005), "Kerala Human Development Report", UNDP.

Uppal, V. (2009), "Is the NREGS a Safety Net for Children"?, (unpublished thesis), Oxford, University of Oxford.

Ushadevi, B. (2010), "Achieving Millennium Development Goals through Kudumbashree", Study on Venganoor Panchayat, Kerala, unpublished Ph.D. dissertation, Gandhigram Rural University, Gandhigram, Tamil Nadu, India.

Vaidyanathan, A. (1994b), "Employment Situation: Some Emerging Perspectives", *Economic and Political Weekly*, December 10.

Vanaik, A. and Siddharth (2008), "Bank Payments: End of Corruption in NREGA", *Economic and Political Weekly*, 43(17), August 5.

Vijayan, A. (2007), "A Decade of Gender Mainstreaming in Local Governance in Kerala" in Oommen, M.A. (eds.), A Decade of Decentralization in Kerala Experience and Lessons, Institute of Social Sciences, New Delhi.

Vijayakumar, B. and S.N. Thomas (2008), "Governance, Institutions and National Rural Employment Guarantee Scheme", International Conference on NREGS in India: Impacts and Implementation Experiences, New Delhi, September.

Von Braun, Joachim (1995), "Employment for Poverty Reduction and Food Security: Concepts, Research Issues and Overview", 'in Von Braun (ed.), Employment for Poverty Reduction and Food Security, International Food Policy Research Institute, Washington D.C.

Weinberger, Katinka (2000), "Women's Participation: An Economic Analysis in Rural Chad and Pakistan", Peter Lang Europaischer Verlag der Wissenschaften, Frankfurt am Main.

Zachariah, K.C., Mathew, E.T. and S. Irudaya Rajan (2002), Dynamics of Migration in Kerala: Dimensions, Determinants and Consequences, Orient Longman Pvt. Ltd., London.

Index

Index